# Mary Immaculate
# In The Divine Plan

Michael D. Meilach O.F.M.

Preface by J. B. Carol, O.F.M.

Michael Glazier, Inc.
Wilmington, Delaware

First published in 1981 by
Michael Glazier, Inc.
1210 King Street
Wilmington, DE 19801

Library of Congress Catalog Card Number: 81-80821
International Standard Book Number: 0-89453-258-8

Cover: Virgin With Flowers by Derain

Printed in the United States of America

# THE AUTHOR

Franciscan Michael D. Meilach is on the faculty of the Department of Philosophy at Siena College, Loudonville, New York. He is well-known for his editorship of *The Cord* magazine, and first established his reputation as a writer with the publication of *The Primacy of Christ*. He is widely respected as a theologian.

# CONTENTS

# EDITORIAL NOTE

THE PLACE of the Mother of Jesus in Christian thought and life is receiving revigorated attention in many respects, catechetically, liturgically and ecumenically. Publisher Michael Glazier is bringing out a new series, *The Mary Library*, on the Blessed Virgin in response to the growing interest in her. Very competent authors have been invited to explore important aspects of the mystery of Mary, Mother of Christ, model of the Church. These compact studies bring out the special significance of the Mother of Jesus in God's plan of mercy.

Gospel woman of faith, Mary of Nazareth is the splendid achievement of the saving grace of God; perfect follower of Jesus her Son; and, in the power of his Spirit, sharer still in the triumph of the Risen Christ by her abiding role of intercession in the communion of saints. Many dynamic movements in present-day Christianity have a Marian dimension, for example, charismatic interest in the bond between Mary and the Holy Spirit, and ecumenical concern for Mary's role in Church unity. These and other lively theological themes are being considered in *The Mary Library*.

Eamon R. Carroll, O. Carm.
General Editor of *The Mary Library*

# PREFACE

WRITING TO THE Christian community of Ephesus, the Apostle of the Gentiles reminds them that the riches of Christ are "unfathomable." He refers to the mysterious designs "hidden" in God (Eph. 3:8-9). And so they are indeed. That, however, has hardly dampened the perennial curiosity of theologians as they wander through the realm of divine secrets always searching for new and richer insights.

A concrete example of this type of noble endeavor is the book we are honored to present to our cultured readers. Its author undertakes a serious inquiry into the singular place held by Christ and Mary in the overall plan of God relative to the universe. Father Meilach is well equipped to launch the investigation. His solid philosophical and theological training comes through—crystal clear—on every page. His several previous essays on the precise topic of the present brochure eminently qualify him as an expert in the field.

The process adopted by the author is an orderly and reflective analysis of theological data regarding the final cause of the creation of the universe and the logical "moments" in the predestination of intelligent creatures, leading us step by step to a coherently structured synthesis in which Christ and Mary emerge as holding an absolute and universal primacy over the rest of creation. Precisely because of this unique primacy championed by the author, the conclusion is reached that the Savior and His Mother must have been predestined first, and hence independently of Adam's fall. Flowing logically from the above is the further conclusion that Christ and Mary are the secondary final, efficient (meritorious), and exemplary cause of all God's works *ad extra*.

But the author is not satisfied with setting forth the broad outlines of his thesis. He lucidly expands on its obvious implications regarding a wide range of questions such as the fundamental principle of Mariology, our Lady's intimate share in the Savior's redemptive mission, the controversy over the so-called "debt of sin," and so forth. In this connection it is particularly refreshing to read that the dogma of the Immaculate Conception, proclaimed by Pope Pius IX in 1854, will never be fully understood until it is envisioned within the context of our Lady's predestination totally unconnected with our first parents' prevarication.

In our judgment, the Scotistic perspective pervading the entire volume is developed with such clarity and cogency that fair-minded readers will find its presentation highly satisfactory and rewarding. The premises on which that perspective is based are not only rooted in the Catholic conscience and vouched for in Sacred Scripture, they are admirably illuminated by the light of human reason as well.

While we congratulate our distinguished colleague and confrere on his latest achievement, we express the sincere hope that the intriguing thesis of his book will find widespread and enthusiastic acceptance among our English-speaking coreligionists. It richly deserves it.

J. B. Carol, O.F.M., S.T.D.
Feast of the Presentation of Our Lady, 1980

# INTRODUCTION

AS THE INTRODUCTORY VOLUME in a new series of books on the Blessed Virgin Mary, this essay is intended to "set the stage," as it were, for the drama to unfold in subsequent volumes. Set the stage: another, more literal way to express this is, "establish the context."

For some people Mariology may seem to be a self-enclosed area of study and Marian devotion an independent, isolated set of pious practices—both of them devoid of any connection with the larger scheme of things: creation, human destiny in general, and human experience in a social and technological milieu.

To view our Lady this way, however—to think that Mariology and Marian devotion can subsist or even make much sense in a vacuum—is to be content with an impoverished understanding of God's unified creative plan and seriously to underestimate the centrality of Mary in that plan.

We intend, then, to "set the stage." This will involve combining, in a way that is not very common in recent Mariological writing, philosophical reflection and theological doctrine. The central presupposition throughout the essay is that nature was made for grace, our rational minds for revelation; and so there is a need to ground Marian doctrine as well as our entire theological appreciation of the divine plan in a clear understanding of what it means for God to create at all and how, as the supremely intelligent Agent, he ought to be conceived as ordering the various elements of his creative plan.

The notorious question of the so-called "God of the philosophers" is therefore rejected. According to it, philosophy argues for the existence of some cold, abstract principle which cannot subsequently be identified with the loving God of Abraham, Isaac, and Jacob, the Father of our Lord Jesus Christ. If the early portions of this book seem to be concerned with preponderantly philosophical concepts, it should be borne in mind that these concepts are absolutely needed for later use in reflecting more theologically on the place of Jesus and Mary in creation.

Our progress through the volume will be a gradual one, as we move from a series of reflections on God as Creator, to the notion of predestination in general as a fundamental feature of his creative act, and only then on to explicitly Christological and Mariological considerations.

The book ends, not with the general reflections on creation and predestination—even as applied specifically to our Lady—but with the quite specific doctrine of Mary's Immaculate Conception. The inclusion of that doctrine within this introductory volume is, far from being gratuitous or arbitrary, or even merely fitting, actually designed to show the intimate link between the Immaculate Conception as defined by Pope Pius IX and the absolute and eternal predestination of our Lady.

*Chapter I*

*Creation*

# Chapter I

# CREATION

"WE BELIEVE in one God, the Father, the Almighty, Maker of heaven and earth . . . ." Thus do we Christians profess a belief which, however strongly we hold it, we rarely stop to consider reflectively. Such reflective consideration does, admittedly, have to be somewhat abstract and difficult in some of its aspects, but the effort brings with it rich rewards. The apparently "cold" philosophical interpretation of this first article of our Creed, when duly appropriated and savoured, yields rich spiritual nourishment.

As is often the case, such positive benefits are impeded by obstacles in the form of misconceptions which must be cleared away. To understand properly the concept of creation, we have to get rid of two notions that are, unfortunately, all too common: (1) that the business of philosophical speculation on God is primarily to "prove" the existence of an absent God, whose creative activity would be known only indirectly, as a conclusion from the existence of his "effects," creatures; and (2) that one must somehow take a mental journey backward into the past and discover the Creator at the beginning of a long sequence of events.

According to the first misconception, philosophers prove God's existence the way the man in the street would infer from the existence of a broken store window and missing merchandise the earlier visit of a thief, now nowhere to be seen. Nowhere, perhaps, has this mistake been more resolutely exposed than in John E. Smith's fine work, *Experience and God*, where all such "proofs" are shown to contain their conclusion in their starting point: our human life lived in the presence of God our Creator.[1] In our intuition of our own frailty, our dependence and lack of any reason within ourselves why we should exist rather than not exist, we experience the Ground of our existence, who secures us in being, graciously and powerfully and lovingly communicating to us all that we have and are. In our awareness of life's purposiveness—that somehow, even when things seem to be going all wrong, at bottom it all makes sense and life *is* going somewhere—we likewise discern the strong, loving hand of our Creator leading us in his wisdom toward the fulfillment for which we so ardently thirst. And in our deeply rooted sense of responsibility for our actions—in the faithful accomplishment of our duty no less than in the guilt-laden experience of failure and rebellion, we know at first hand the presence of the glorious, all-knowing and all-just Lord of heaven and earth. It is, then, not primarily outward, toward things—objects—that we must turn to discover God's presence, but inward, to that profound depth of our being where the Most High dwells and invites us to maintain with him a constant dialogue of the purest personal love.

The second misconception, we said, consists in thinking we have to retrace the world's temporal development to find God at its beginning. This is the well known position of the nineteenth-century "deists," who for one or several reasons of their own wanted nothing to do with a present, personal Creator to whom human beings would be responsible. But to think of creation this way is totally to misunderstand its essential meaning. Created, finite, dependent being cannot be set adrift, as it were, on its own as though it needed no further support once it was brought into being, any more than a chandelier, once attached to the ceiling, can thenceforth be detached and expected to sustain itself in midair. If, as is the case, we depend at each moment and in a total way upon our Creator, then he is to be found precisely thus—at each moment, in the present moment, holding us firmly in his grasp. Otherwise we should simply cease to exist—vanish without a trace.

The mystery we are meditating on is, then, a dynamic, immediate, and present communication of our whole reality from the prodigal hands of our Creator. Hands? Of course not. Maybe we never really adverted to this question or felt the need explicitly to answer it; but were we actually asked, we could quickly enough reply that God does not fashion the universe as a cobbler does a pair of shoes: pick up some material, labor for a while on it, and turn it out, a finished product. But is it equally easy to say what he *does* do?

Here we find ourselves confronted with the perennial, but today especially acute, problem of the meaningfulness of religious language. In the early part of this century there arose a school of thought called logical positivism, which was later succeeded by the still widely prevalent approach known as linguistic analysis, or analytic philosophy.[2] One of the major concerns of this entire movement is the "criterion for meaningfulness" of any sentence. At first it was maintained that one must be able to verify a statement for it to be meaningful—i.e., set up a concrete experiential situation which would show the statement true by sensibly perceptible illustration. When that basic principle itself was shown to violate its own rule, the philosophers turned to a "falsification" principle; now one had to show what kind of situation would prove a sentence, not true, but false. If God is a loving Father, e.g., could we possibly have the amount of suffering we do in a world he creates and sustains with infinite power and goodness? Because believers would not admit that the existence of any degree of evil disproves the statement that "God exists," or would admit that any conceivable situation would disprove this statement, their religious utterances were declared "meaningless."

Other members of the linguistic movement then pointed out that language has different functions, only one of which is strictly speaking "cognitive." Restricting the cognitive use of language (in virtue of which it gives information about the nature of things) to the sciences, they assigned to religious language an "emotive" character. It tells us nothing about the way things are, they insisted, but expresses how *I* want to see them, the kind of life I have opted to live.

The alternative to this agnostic position is the venerable doctrine of analogy. We know that God cannot, on the one hand, be exactly like us in any of his characteristics; his infinity, eternal self-identify, and absolute necessity all mean that he "has it together," to use a strikingly fitting contemporary slang expression, in an absolutely perfect unity quite impossible for any creature. On the other hand, however, it is wrong to conclude from this that nothing whatever can be known about God—that the supremely personal Other with whom we enter into conversation in the depths of our being is so completely unlike us that we can say nothing meaningful about him. The reason we can speak meaningfully of him is that any cause must have what it communicates to the effect it produces. (You can't give what you haven't got!) If it be objected that the shoe doesn't get its quality of leatherness, the rubberness of its heel, etc., from the shoemaker, we can easily see the truth of such an observation. But the cobbler uses leather and rubber already available; no one credits him with making the materials. What he does give the shoe (its pattern and whatever else makes for its utility precisely as a shoe) does come from his own creativity—from his mental conception of the product and his labor in assembling it. In the case of divine creation, though, there is no material already available. If God himself does not possess a given quality, there is no way that his creature can have it.

Are we then to say that God is yellow because there are yellow things like chickens and daffodils? Obviously not—a being must be material and hence limited to be yellow. All we can say is that God must have the power to produce yellow objects, not that he himself is yellow. In technical terms, yellowness is said to be a "mixed perfection," one that implies limitation; and God can possess it only "virtually." (The Latin *virtus* means power, and hence the term connotes the power to produce the quality in question.)

We can easily see the difference, however, between qualities like yellowness that can exist only in limited beings, and others like intelligence and love, which in their essential meaning connote no such limitation. True, we human beings possess intelligence in a less than perfect manner. Not only do we not know everything, that is, but even the knowledge we do have is gained by a slow and sometimes laborious process. Not so with God, whose infinite perfection means that his knowledge is instantaneous as well as comprehensive. Qualities like intelligence, therefore, are called "pure" rather than "mixed," because they contain no admixture of imperfection or limitation in their essential meaning, regardless of their actual limitation as we creatures possess them; and God is said to possess them "formally" rather than virtually. (The Latin *forma* means intrinsic actuality.)

Analogy can thus be seen to mean that as our Cause, God really ("formally") possesses all the pure perfections, not as we do but in an infinitely perfect way. His intelligence and his love are not exactly like ours (the terms denoting them do not mean exactly the same thing in his case and in ours). They are not, in other words, applied univocally to him and to us. But neither are they something utterly unrelated to ours (the terms denoting them do not have completely unrelated meanings, like "bark" applied to the skin of a tree and "bark" applied to the voice of a dog). They are not, in other words, applied equivocally to him and to us. Rather, both God and we possess these perfections, but in a manner which is partly the same (the root meaning) and partly different (the way in which we possess them).

Needless to say, the foregoing discussion of religious language was not a speculative exercise for its own sake. It was needed to justify the ensuing explanation of creation in the face of persistent contemporary denials that we can speak meaningfully of transcendence. Unless these denials can be convincingly refuted, not only is it impossible to continue with our exposition of creation in the largely philosophical framework of the present chapter, but what we shall have to say later on regarding the theological conception of God's creative and redemptive plan will also be dismissed as pretentious ventures beyond what is open to the human mind.

To create is to be an agent, a doer, a cause, a producer. To gain some understanding of the divine act of creation, therefore, we look to features of God—pure perfections— which are not merely qualities, such as mercy, justice, or beauty, but actions. From our knowledge of ourselves as persons and agents, as well as from our personal encounter with the divine Other, we then come to realize that to create, for God, can mean nothing else than to know himself as imitable in a finite way—in his created image and likeness—and to will effectively that such an image and likeness actually exist. Whereas our finite minds come to know actually existing realities and possess true knowledge when they conform to those realities, God's mind actually gives meaning to the realities he knows as imitations of himself, and *they* are said to be "true" in that they conform to his creative knowledge. Whereas our finite wills come to love actually existing realities we realize will benefit us, God's will actually gives to the realities he creates whatever goodness they possess, and they are said to be good precisely in that they exist and to the extent that they do exist, that they participate in and imitate God's perfections.

So creation means simply this, that the infinitely perfect Creator knows himself as imitable in a finite way and wills that such limited realities actually exist. It also means that this creative knowing and loving take place "substantially" —in their fullness—at the very moment when any creature exists. God does not "conserve" in a subordinate way what he has already "created" in the past, the way a cook simmers soup which has already boiled sufficiently. Creation is a making-be-now.

The obvious question that must be met at this point is: why? Why does God create at all? Here again, at a new level, there arises a persistent diffidence. The question seems, not merely impertinent, but quite unanswerable from our human viewpoint. God is, after all, infinite (the term has been used often in the foregoing paragraphs). And what can we know or say about the infinite? After all, nothing in our day-to-day, secular existence is infinite; we are not in the habit of coming upon infinite things alongside slightly smaller, finite ones. Are we then simply to abandon any effort to fathom the motive for creation?

What has been said about the doctrine of analogy is pertinent here too. Resisting the tendency often encountered

among our contemporaries, we should avoid selling ourselves short and unduly denigrating the intelligence we
have. Up is up; down, down. There is nothing relative about
that. So is existence positive, its absence negative. Unity,
truth, goodness, beauty: these go with existence and are
positive. Dispersion into multiplicity, falsity, evil, ugliness:
these go with non-being and are negative. This is an appeal,
ultimately, to the principle of intelligibility: that being as
such is knowable. Either we make no claim to know anything (in which case we are sure we do not know!), or we
admit that the mind is made to know, and we assume the
responsibility for following out the implications of what we
discover—all the way, as far as careful, critical reasoning
will lead us.

We must not flinch, therefore, in the face of the heady
task of trying to plumb the depths of the infinite; for we are
made in its likeness. We are so made that our minds are
open to pure infinity and our hearts endowed with a craving
for it. We shall be restless—incomplete and unfulfilled—
until our hearts rest in it.

Why, then, creation? Why does God create at all? We
must begin our answer to this question in this chapter,
but we cannot complete it here. That is to say, our aim is
ultimately to show that creation makes full, complete sense
only in Jesus Christ and that his Blessed Mother therefore
plays a centrally important role, not merely in our spiritual
life and in our redemption, but in creation itself. Unless
this perspective is to appear totally foreign to our concrete
human, experiential life, however, we must first be clear
about what rational reflection discloses about God's motive
for creating.

Every agent acts for some purpose—some goal or end to
be attained. Non-rational creatures are so made that they
automatically and necessarily seek their natural goal.

Water flows down, not up; bees gather honey and do not build dams; beavers build dams and do not sink roots into the earth. We human beings are different. We do have our natural physical and biological processes, true, so that our stomachs, for example, have no choice but to digest food that they receive. But we do not refer to such necessary, automatic functions as specifically human. Rather, we speak of a truly human act when we are aware of the various possibilities and, understanding the value of the several courses of action open to us, we select one specific goal to be achieved and take the steps necessary to achieve it.

Similarly—analogously but not univocally—God is an Agent. Supremely intelligent, he knows in a single flash all the implications and all the values of various courses of action. He too, therefore, chooses among these courses of action; he has a goal, and he takes the steps needed to attain it. But his action is, we have said, only analogous to ours—not precisely the same, nor totally different so as to be unintelligible to us. His own inner life, to begin with, is a single, eternal, absolutely perfect self-knowledge and self-love, both of which are so perfect that they result in Persons co-equal, "one in being" with himself. But when it comes to other actions, we cannot say that God is necessitated to perform them as he is to live his own divine life. His infinity and necessity preclude dependence upon anything outside himself; and any end of goal is something upon which an agent in a real sense depends: it governs him, determines his actions. Since nothing outside God can govern him, reduce him as it were to a state of dependence, his motive for creating cannot be situated outside himself at all, but must somehow be found within his own independent, self-sufficient nature.

This teaching was commonplace before the post-Vatican II upheaval, but it is surprising how much resistance it meets with today. There seems to be a concerted effort underway to reduce God to human proportions—to get the kind of handle on him that the ancient Hebrews learned the hard way they could not get. In the process philosophy of Alfred North Whitehead, e.g., we find the strange doctrine that God and the world need one another equally and are mutually dependent.[3] And several Catholic theologians who should know better have danced to this pernicious tune.[4] Let us repeat it: God is the Creator; all else is contingent, totally dependent in its very being upon his creative act.

God's motive for creating is, then, to be sought within his own infinitely loving nature. The medievals liked to use the neo-Platonic principle that "goodness is diffusive of itself" to explain why the self-sufficient and all-perfect Absolute would want to share with others the perfections he himself enjoyed from all eternity. That principle in its original form implied a certain necessity: the Good *had* to overflow by its very nature. In its Christian application, however, it was carefully nuanced to mean that the all-perfect Godhead, while necessarily overflowing within the trinitarian circle, *freely* decides to share the bliss of his life with creatures who have no claim of any sort on his creativity. The nuancing is crucial: were creatures necessary, they too would be divine; God would be conceived as dispersing his own being into a degraded multiplicity, and the resulting perspective would be an unintelligible pantheism.

Freely, therefore, and out of pure liberality, God decides in an eternal, timeless decree that there will be creatures mirroring his infinite beauty, each in its finite way exemplifying certain facets of what in the Godhead is limitless unity of perfect, living bliss.

It remains, now, for us to examine the implications of our earlier statement that God is a supremely intelligent Agent who "takes steps" to achieve his goal. Is there a latent contradiction here, in that the eternal Absolute, who utterly transcends time, might be said to take one step after another in establishing a created universe?

As we have seen, creation means both knowing and loving on God's part. To understand the *order* that characterizes creation—the "steps" God takes in accomplishing his creative decree—we need to dwell further on these same divine actions (or better, these aspects of the single, unified divine act which is creation). We have already said that God, as an Agent, acts for an end; now we must add that, like every agent, he works in an orderly way. This means, not that he issues successive decrees, but that there is among the creatures he produces an intelligible order such that the lower, the less perfect, exist for and serve the needs of the higher or more perfect.

Traditionally, theologians have spoken of this order using the metaphor of time, saying that God "first" wills the more perfect creatures and "then" the less perfect. They knew better, of course, than to introduce different temporal stages into God's timeless, eternal decree of creation; but they insisted that this way of expressing the point clarifies it for our human understanding. They had a good precedent for this procedure, moreover, in the Genesis accounts of creation.

The discussion so far has been, in the main, philosophical rather than theological. That is, it has been about the creation of a universe known from experience to be contingent and therefore created by a necessary Cause whose activity consists in knowledge and love. Even within this strictly philosophical framework, we can discern what must be the order in God's creative plan simply by reflecting on the various creatures known to us in our experience.

Thus, whatever may be said for the intelligence of dolphins or for the love many of us bear for our pets—dogs and cats—we know that dolphins have never produced a civilization and that no dog or cat has ever written a novel or created a Rembrandt. Again, we can forestall objections about extraterrestrial intelligent creatures by pointing out that we are dealing with creatures we have experienced. No judgment is being ventured here about the existence of others we have not yet encountered. Certainly there is nothing impossible, *a priori*, about their existence, and should any such creatures exist, provision for them can easily be made in the perspective outlined here. If they are intelligent in a fashion superior to ours, they would rank above us in the creative order; if of basically the same nature as we, with us; and if of an inferior nature, below us.

This first chapter has been a mainly philosophical discussion of creation: its meaning as a free and orderly divine action and as a general framework within which to situate the roles played by Jesus Christ and his Blessed Mother in the divine plan. Crucial to an understanding of their role, however, is the notion of predestination: God's special provision for the ultimate fulfillment of his rational creatures.

*Chapter II*
*Predestination*

# Chapter II
# PREDESTINATION

"PREDESTINATION," etymologically, evidently has to do with a "destining beforehand." Within the purely philosophical framework elaborated in the preceding chapter, we could easily show that the intelligent Creator is provident toward his rational creatures—that it would make no sense to make human beings able to know and love him unless he planned from the outset ("beforehand") to lead them to that very goal ("destiny").

But it is not in this purely natural, philosophical sense that predestination has traditionally been treated by Catholic writers. In fact, as we shall see in later chapters, even creation itself is not a purely natural, philosophical matter; it is transformed through and through by the supernatural order so that it becomes something quite other than it would have been in an economy without provision for the Incarnation. Predestination is a supernatural affair, then: divine Providence itself, exercised toward those who actually attain supernatural salvation.[1]

We may begin our exploration of predestination by pointing out that God wills, not only that certain chosen individuals be saved, but that all human beings reach the supernatural destiny that is union with him in an ever-lasting ecstasy of knowledge and love. This desire of God, called his "general salvific will," is put into effect by his act of predestination, which includes not only a decree that people be saved, but the provision of the means necessary for this salvation.

It may be asked, in view of the possibility that not everyone is actually saved (and the certainty that some angels are not saved), whether this will or desire on God's part is to be taken seriously. The answer is an unqualified *yes*. The Church has emphatically rejected the teaching of the Calvinists and the Jansenists, among others, who maintained that God absolutely and with no consideration of people's merit selects a certain few individuals whom he marks for salvation while decreeing that others will be forever damned.

The means God provides for everyone's salvation include that share in his own life which is known as sanctifying grace, a special care lavished on each individual known as particular providence, the precious gift of perseverance amid life's constant distractions and temptations.

Now we know that it is possible for individuals to refuse these divine gifts and hence not attain the end to which they have been predestined. Some kind of distinction therefore must be made and indeed has traditionally been made by theologians. There is "complete" predestination and "incomplete" predestination. Only for those who actually do attain eternal life is predestination said to be complete. Nor is this to be conceived, as it was by the Pelagians, as merely a matter of God's knowledge; it involves his will as well.

Now we have the paradox bluntly stated: God wants everyone to be saved; indeed, he so predestines them, intending them to attain salvation and providing all the necessary means for them to do so. Yet he not only knows, but even wills that some not be saved! Evidently we need a closer look at this divine will; we need to do some more distinguishing if we expect to make sense of the mystery of predestination.

Earlier, in our discussion of the order in creation, we saw that even though God acts in a simple, timeless decree, we human beings find it helpful to analyze that single decree metaphorically in temporal terms. What we thus place "before" another reality is actually, literally, more perfect than that other reality or is ordered to that other reality as means to end. When we describe God's actual willing of those realities, we term the various "stages" of his will "moments." In this context of predestination too, theologians distinguish "moments" in an effort to resolve the paradox with which we have just found ourselves confronted.

God is pictured as saying to himself, "first," "I want to save this man"; this first "moment" expresses his general salvific will in such a way that it is concretely applied to a specific individual. Next, he is seen as selecting the various means to implement that will: grace, the gift of perseverance, eternal life. In a third phase or "moment," God is said to take account of the person's merit or lack of it—i.e., co-operation with or rejection of grace. Finally, assuming the person has in fact cooperated and thus merited, God confers upon that person everlasting life and glory.

The whole process, it should be made clear, is absolutely gratuitous—a sheer gift from God in no way attainable by the human person's own unaided efforts, in no way due to him as a creature, and in no way flowing from any aspect of his own nature or activities. These facts are due to the supernatural character of the goal actually planned for us by God, in virtue of which there exists no purely natural order. But then how, in such a context, can we speak of "merit" at all? It makes sense to speak of merit, as long as we understand that the very possibility of meriting is itself a gift—part of the larger, total gift which is predestination. Merit results from the creature's free cooperation with grace; but the grace itself, as well as the freedom to co-operate with it, is wholly from God.

This division of God's act of predestination into "moments" enables us to pinpoint one of them as the crucial element with which to resolve our paradox: the third "moment," which is human merit. Thomistic theologians have for the most part maintained that the final decree of glory takes place "before" any consideration of the person's merit. The so-called "Congruist" school, on the other hand, has maintained that the final decree of glory for an individual takes place "after" consideration of merits. Here we see the importance of understanding correctly the metaphorical device of "moments," because it cannot, obviously, be a question of God's performing one act "after" another. What is meant is that the decree of glory is *conditioned upon* the human person's cooperation with divine grace.

There has never been a definitive decision by the Church in favor of one or the other of these two schools. The Thomistic school has this in its favor, that it seems to give full weight to the divine omnipotence, envisaging the decree of glory for an individual as absolute. God infallibly attains, with no interference from or dependence upon any creature, what he freely decides to accomplish in his creation. In all candor, however, it is diffcult to see how such a solution avoids the Jansenist and Calvinist implication that God absolutely predestines one individual to glory and another to damnation. In the Molinist or Congruist position, on the other hand, we seem to face the anomaly of the almighty Creator depending upon his creature's free decision for the accomplishment of his divine plan.

The key to resolving this question seems to lie in a proper understanding of the profound mystery of human, created freedom. Surely God is himself supremely free, absolute, and independent; but in that sovereign freedom he can decide to condition a decree of his upon the fulfillment of certain requirements by the free creature. To say this is in no way to imply an absolute dependence of Creator upon creature. Nothing whatever that the creature has, or does, is in the last analysis wholly his own; everything comes from God. Even in the case of free choice, the action of deciding is not wholly the human person's. A better way to put it would be that it *is* wholly the human person's from one standpoint, that of secondary causality; but that is the point: such causality is in itself derived, wholly dependent upon God's creative act so that the decision is also, in a more profound and ultimate sense, God's action.

How, then, is it free? The creature cannot produce being or reality from nothingness—cannot add to God's creation. The good act which constitutes a cooperation with grace must therefore be seen as wholly due to God's creative power, which the creature has not obstructed—more positively, has freely allowed to attain its intended goal. The evil act, however—refusal to cooperate with grace—is not, precisely in its deformed character *as evil*, anything positive at all. As we remarked in the preceding chapter, existence, truth, unity, and goodness are the positive realities, and non-being, falsity, dispersion into multiplicity, and evil are the negative. What the sinning creature does, then, is with God's "permission"—not to be understood as approval, but as a sort of resigned, sorrowful non-interference—to "nihilate."[2] That is, the free creature has it within his own power to stop the divine creative activity "in its tracks"—to undo being, to open up a gaping hole or fissure in creation. God wills the good, but the human person is free to prevent its attainment. And thus by pure negation and with God's consent (implicit in the granting of free will to the creature), his general salvific will which certainly applied "antecedently" to this hapless creature is rejected. The act of predestination to glory, dependent through God's free decree upon the creature's acquiescence, is not actually fulfilled.

Thus is our paradox resolved: "antecedently," God does will the salvation of each and every human person, but "consequently," taking into account the person's refusal of God's loving offer, he not only knows (as the Pelagians assert) but actually wills the sinner's damnation. Far from being petty, spiteful, or vindictive as an anthropomorphic understanding of the question might suggest, God is supremely just in repudiating the sinner who has first repudiated him. He cannot do otherwise, because to force salvation on one who does not want it, is to undo the creature's freedom. More than that, it is an impossibility— a contradiction in terms.

In the case of the individual who does cooperate with the grace given him, however, God's decree does attain its end, which is eternal life for the creature. And in such a case, God is said, in the traditional technical term, to "predefine" all that person's salutary acts—all the actions which constitute cooperation with grace and merit of salvation.

Here again, we must call attention to a divergence between Thomists and Congruists. Consistent with their basic position on predestination, the Thomists maintain that God foreordains each specific act that the creature will perform in a manner that is not merely direct and immediate, but even "efficacious"— i.e., effective in such a way that the creature would seem to be wholly determined, antecedently to any choice of his own, to perform the act. The Molinists, similarly consistent, do not attribute the final characteristic of "efficacity" to this act of God's will.

## Creation, Predestination, and Process Philosophy

Before concluding this preliminary, general exposition of creation and predestination and moving on to its Christological and Mariological applications, we must pause briefly to consider one of today's most influential schools of thought, process philosophy, to take some measure of its implications for Christology and Mariology.

There are many and widely varied schools of philosophy today, of course, and so it may be asked, why single out process thought for consideration in this volume of a Mariology series? The reason may be stated in two parts. First, it is the only significant contemporary school of philosophy other than neoscholasticism which explicitly professes to supply a metaphysics—an explanation of the structure of reality. Other schools, admittedly just as influential, restrict their considerations to human consciousness or the use of language. But, secondly, what Christian theology has always sought from rational analysis is an explanation of the actual nature of the realities involved in its doctrine: God, human beings, the angels, the material world, and, above all, the God-man and his blessed mother. This is why Catholic as well as Protestant theologians have so eagerly adopted process categories for theological use: process philosophy affords them a metaphysics that appears to them to be more modern, more applicable to the world as we know it today than the earlier scholastic philosophy elaborated on the ancient foundations supplied by Plato and Aristotle.

Contemporary process thought is of two main types: Whiteheadian and Teilhardian. Both share a quintessentially modern concern for the importance of temporal development and for the interrelatedness of all that exists. On both counts they constitute a reaction against the extreme forms (really distortions) of traditional Greek and scholastic thought. The older theology, process thinkers feel, conceived of God as too remote, not sufficiently involved in the world; and in addition they characterize it as too static, with too little attention paid to historical development, to the gradual emergence of new elements in the creative process. But for all their similarity as regards their basic thrust and purpose, the two schools differ radically in the remedy they propose for what they see as the defects of neoscholastic or "classical" philosophy and theology.

Whiteheadian process thought derives its name from Alfred North Whitehead (1861-1947), the Anglo-American physicist and mathematician turned philosopher, whose mature philosophical writings appeared in the late 1920s and early 1930s. Bringing to the task of creating a contemporary metaphysics the physical principles of quantum and relativity which he had himself helped to develop, Whitehead set forth a highly technical and extremely complex perspective in which every reality is at its heart a private, microscopic pulse of value-feeling or experience. Every reality—God as much as the most trivial "puff of existence," in Whitehead's striking phrase—is thus in process of becoming. More accurately, the sense-perceptible and enduring realities we experience are huge aggregates of temporal series of such processes. Infinitesimal in both size and function, each micro-process perishes as soon as it has become what it has set out to become, and a new one arises in its place.

Whitehead's followers differ on the question of how literally this description can be applied to God. Some maintain, following Whitehead's own apparent position, that God is a single such process, everlasting in its "concrescence"—growth or development—whereas others feel

constrained by the logic of Whitehead's system to revise
that teaching and maintain that God, no less than every
other reality, is a series of feeling-pulses, each of which
perishes in successive instants. For the latter, God is a
"temporal series" of the so-called "actual occasions" said
by Whitehead to constitute all of reality.[3]

We cannot, of course, go further into the complexities
of Whitehead's perspective. For present purposes, we want
only to highlight the consequences for theology of his
characterization of God. The most important of these
concern the two subjects we have treated: creation and
predestination.

In his concern to avoid the "wholly other," allegedly
static, infinite God of classical theism, Whitehead deliber-
ately depicts God as finite, growing, developing. And to
guarantee the reality of human freedom and of the emergence of real "novelty" in the world process, he denies to
God any actual infinity of perfection, especially omnipotence. God's creative activity is restricted to the proposal
of possibilities for other realities, which then accept and
reject what they will with no other consequence than the
attainment of a less ideal fruition for their momentary,
fleeting "satisfaction" or destiny. Those realities are not
created from nothing by God, moreover, but literally
create themselves. The world is necessary, has always
existed; and it has no specific goal toward which it would
be moving but is rather in an open-ended process of development without end. The world and God are mutually
dependent, so that God needs the world as much as the
world needs God for their common growth and "enjoyment" of existence.[4]

The human soul too, is for Whitehead an "actual occasion." It is the dominant one in the human organism,
and it is said to wander within the empty spaces of the

brain. But Whitehead's followers face the same difficulty regarding the soul's duration as they do with regard to God's. Some consistently maintain that as God is one enduring entity, so is the soul, while others with equal consistency maintain that both God and the soul are temporal series of instantaneously self-creating and perishing pulses of experience. In either case, however, one can hardly speak of predestination in the traditional Christian sense. If God does not bestow existence, he can hardly predestine the self-creative human soul, the existence of which after death is in any case highly problematic in Whiteheadian process thought.[5]

The Christology based on this metaphysics is at least implicitly adoptionist: that is, Jesus is depicted as a human person who is extraordinarily receptive to God's proffered ideals—more so, for Christian Whiteheadians, than any other human person—but only in degree, not in kind. The essence of classical teaching on the Incarnation, painstakingly worked out at the Councils of Chalcedon and Ephesus, is the union of two natures—divine and human—in the single Person of the Incarnate Word. But since one of the primary features of classical thought repudiated by Whiteheadian philosophy is the notion of stable natures or essences, there is no way to express the traditional doctrine of the Incarnation in Whiteheadian terms. Jesus becomes, as was said above, different from other human beings only in degree, not in kind. And if anything special is to be said for his Mother, it too must involve only a matter of degree; she cannot be said to participate in an order unique in kind, as we shall see was the case in classical theology.

Teilhardian process thought is quite different from that of Whitehead. The French Jesuit Pierre Teilhard de Chardin (1881-1955) did share Whitehead's passion for reintegrating what he felt had been broken asunder by the older theology. As a priest, he had the usual full philosophical and theological education, but he went on to become a paleontologist by profession, and much of his life's work can be seen as a sustained effort to combine in one rich vision the viewpoints of the philosopher, the theologian, and the scientist.

The key notion from science is that of evolution: the entire universe is like a growing tree on which newer and higher forms of reality emerge with the passage of time. This takes place, not in a continuous fashion but by "quantum leaps" as the inorganic "boils over" into the organic, and the organic into the spiritual (all, of course, under God's constant creative activity; but the scientist cannot, as such, take that into account).[6]

If there is an equally fundamental notion from philosophy, it is that of uniting love—love which causes union. God is envisaged as creating from nothing, at the beginning, an indifferentiated multiplicity, and love is said to be the force which the Creator uses to increase union and complexity as the evolutionary process continues.[7]

Theologically, Jesus Christ is the center of the entire Teilhardian vision. "Christ the Evolver" is the axis of evolution and its goal. At the world's final consummation the Lord's Body will be complete; he will be "all in all," having drawn all things to himself as the world's Omega Point.[8]

Teilhard's system thus differs more from Whitehead's than it does (at least in the crucial area of theological orthodoxy) from classical Catholic theology. It involves no repudiation of stable natures, and it implies no introduction of becoming (change, development, growth) into the divine nature. On the other hand, those who are convinced that science has contributed something important to their worldview with the theory of evolution are enabled to translate a fully orthodox Catholic outlook into modern process categories. It certainly may be disputed whether classical theology actually portrayed God as remote or uninvolved, as process theologians claim. But there are many people for whom the conception of creation as a gradual unification of the universe—as a constant tending of the evolutionary tree, as it were, by the divine Gardener—may be at least psychologically preferable to the classical concept of "first Cause."

Add to this primary advantage of compatibility with orthodox doctrine the Christocentric emphasis and well known Marian piety of Teilhard,[9] and the version of process thought to which his original genius gave rise is easily seen to be far more acceptable for Catholic theology than the Whiteheadian approach. Indeed, it can even be said to be positively helpful for Catholic theology, as long as one is careful to discount the many extreme statements in which Teilhard gives such vehement expression to his love for the material universe that he sounds literally pantheistic.[10] Let us make explicit in summary form the implications of the Teilhardian system outlined above for the doctrines of creation and predestination.

With regard to creation, we have seen that, far from denying the traditional doctrine of creation out of nothing, Teilhard affirms it. In addition, his emphasis on creation as a continuing, evolutionary process helps us to avoid any tendency to deism: to a view in which God would be seen as creating in the past a universe that was "set adrift" to fend for itself, as it were, without God's further involvement. And finally, we may point out that Teilhard's notion of creation as Christogenesis—the bringing to completion of the Lord's fullness over the entire evolutionary process—accords splendidly with the Christological emphasis we shall present in the next chapter, according to which the entire universe has been created in, through, and for the Incarnate Word, Jesus Christ.

The optimism inherent in Teilhard's evolutionary vision, the thrust of which can be expressed in the slogan, "Ever upward and onward," may at first seem to preclude the integration of traditional teaching on predestination into that vision. This is not the case, however, as Teilhard acknowledges the very real possibility of failure on the part of a large portion of humankind to "move along" with the evolutionary process toward consummation in Christ.[11] Not only is there room for predestination in the traditional sense in Teilhard's thought, therefore, but that notion receives an even greater prominence than in classical theology because of the dynamic emphasis inherent in creative evolution. The sense of movement, of progress into the future, pervades all of Teilhard's writings, and God is constantly envisaged as the Mover guiding that passage. Each of us is called upon to decide, at every moment, whether we will cooperate with God's gracious invitation, and Teilhard never tires of spelling out the consequences of that decision: eternal life in Christ, or reprobation outside the company of the elect.

*       *       *

In the present chapter we have endeavored to set forth the notion of predestination in general as a framework in which to understand the specific predestination of Jesus Christ and his Blessed Mother. We have seen that it is a sovereign act of God, to be understood as a special aspect of his more general creative plan, and that it presupposes the existence of a supernatural order, not juxtaposed to but rather impregnating what would have been a purely natural order devoid of the "extra," gratuitous sharing of God's own life with his creatures. Finally, we have examined a contemporary alternative to the scholastic, classical philosophical framework so long used by Catholic theologians to systematize their reflections on divine revelation.

We have seen that the process thought of Teilhard de Chardin, unlike that of Alfred North Whitehead, can be used to impart an attractive dynamic emphasis to our understanding of God's creative plan. We do not feel that this newer, process approach has been demonstrated to be "true," so that classical metaphysics would be relegated to the status of an outmoded worldview. On the contrary, the reader should be aware of how much in Teilhard's thought depends on the acceptance of evolution, which responsible scientists are quick to point out is not proven fact, but theory. Our point has not been to force a choice between scholastic and process metaphysics, but only to emphasize what is essential in either for a correct understanding of the divine creative plan and the role played in it by Jesus Christ and the Blessed Virgin Mary.

*Chapter III*
*Jesus Christ in the Divine Plan*

# Chapter III

# JESUS CHRIST IN THE DIVINE PLAN

WHAT MAKES the Blessed Virgin Mary special—unique —is precisely the special and unique relationship she has to her divine Son, the God-man, Jesus Christ. Our progress in this volume toward a consideration of her predestination to be his Mother must therefore continue by way of a discussion of *his* predestination. Only when we have properly understood the place of the incarnate Word in the Father's general creative plan can we proceed to discuss the implications for his Mother.

It may be well, in view of today's confused situation where speculative theological matters are concerned, to repeat and expand what has already been said about the correct understanding of the Incarnation.[1]

The formally defined teaching of the Church, which forms the basis for our reflections in this chapter, is that the eternal Word, the second Person of the Blessed Trinity, assumed to himself a human nature created in time, in such a way that there is no human person corresponding to that human nature. Rather, in this unique case, the human nature subsists wholly in the divine Person. There is, moreover, no fusion of natures so that a third kind of reality would result, other than the strictly divine and the strictly human; nor is there any modification of either nature. Jesus Christ is both true God and true man; one and the same divine Word functions in a completely divine manner in his divine nature and in a fully human way in his human nature.

Not only is this defined teaching invoked here against the subordinationism we said seems to be involved in Whiteheadian Christology, according to which Jesus is not literally God, but its very terminology is to be insisted on, against those who seek to replace the words "person" and "nature" with other terms they consider better adapted to our modern linguistic usages. A few words are in order about each of these claims.

With regard to our opposition to Whiteheadian Christology, we must refer the reader to our review of David R. Griffin's book, *A Process Christology*, and the ensuing discussion of that review with Dr. Griffin for a fuller exposition than is possible here.[2] In the present context it must suffice to point out that Whitehead's metaphysics offers no conceptual tool to portray the union *without fusion*, in a single Person—abiding substantial reality—of pure divinity and pure humanity. The soul of Jesus is either a single concrescing pulse of experience or a series of such pulses, independent, private, and self-creative through the assimilation of the data it chooses from its own past and that of the entire surrounding universe.

With regard to our insistence on the "person-nature" terminology, we are similarly prevented by space limitations from offering a full discussion of the issue and want, instead, to refer the reader to the otherwise superb book of Father Dermot A. Lane, *The Reality of Jesus*, for a first-hand look at what happens when one tries to adopt or invent substitute terminology.[3] The allegation is that "person" and "nature" have so changed in meaning since their use in the conciliar definition on the Incarnation that their use now "tends to create confusion in the mind of modern man."[4] And the catalyst par excellence in this process of change has been modern psychology. We do not want to preclude every possibility that at some future date adequate terms may be found to express the dogma accurately, but we leave it to the reader's judgment whether Father Lane has actually discovered any. We believe, moreover, that effort expended in doing so is better directed toward more substantive problems, because no matter what terms are derived from some area of human experience, the mystery of the Incarnation remains unique, requires some preliminary contextual elucidation, and demands some modification of the primary experiential sense of the words adopted.

Why not, then, retain and carefully define the sense of the time-honored terms, "person" and "nature"? The Person of the Word is simply the "individual divine Substance," and contrary to Father Lane's erroneous assertion, it is precisely what *does* act.[5] The nature, on the other hand, is the intrinsic principle *in virtue of which* the substance or person acts. A swan flies in virtue of its swan-like nature, and human beings think in virtue of their human nature. The whole point of the doctrine of the Incarnation is that Jesus does God-like things in virtue of his divine nature, and man-like things in virtue of his human nature, the Agent being identical in both cases.

The main question we face in the present chapter is, in any event, the place or role of the God-man, Jesus Christ, in the Creator's overall plan for the universe. In other words, we seek to understand the *predestination* of Jesus Christ.

The medieval scholastic theologians speculated with avid interest on this question. The twelfth-century Benedictine monk Rupert of Deutz, e.g., thought the Incarnation too magnificent a work on God's part to have been conditioned on sin,[6] and some decades later the Dominican Albert the Great agreed with him.[7] Albert's renowned disciple Thomas Aquinas adopted the opposite view, however, in his extended discussion of the question, "Would God have become incarnate if man had not sinned?"[8] Oddly enough, Thomas casts some doubt on the seriousness with which we ought to take his reply when he says elsewhere that our finite human minds cannot answer such hypothetical questions.[9] But more interestingly for our purposes, he does introduce into the hypothetical discussion the notion of predestination.[10] But neither he nor anyone else before the Franciscan John Duns Scotus treated the question of our Lord's predestination with quite the subtle insight that Scotus brought to it. We concentrate our own attention, then, on Scotus's analysis.[11]

In its structure, the analysis conforms to the standard methodology used in medieval theological writings. The question is stated, then follow negative answers (objections), then affirmative answers, then the author's own position together with clarification of any obscure points or "doubts," and finally answers to the initial objections.

"Was Christ predestined to be the Son of God?" Scotus asks at the outset. And the negative replies follow immediately: "Not as Son of God was [Jesus] predestined to be the Son of God," because the act of *pre*destination obviously has to precede the event predestined, and as God, the Son has of course always existed. Nor could the Lord have been predestined as man to be the Son of God because he is not, according to the second objection, Son of God precisely insofar as he is man. This initial negative point expressed in two objections comes down, then, to a denial that the Person of Jesus Christ could be predestined, because he exists from all eternity.

On the affirmative side, Scotus cites St. Paul (Rom 1:4) to the effect that "[He who was born] of the seed of David . . . was predestined the Son of God in power."[12] He then moves quickly to elaborate his own position, which comprises (1) the explanation we gave in the preceding chapter, that predestination is to glory and includes the grace and merit implied by that definitive goal, and (2) a discussion of how predestination can possibly apply to a mere nature. Persons, not natures, are the responsible agents who can receive grace, cooperate with it, and attain glory. Scotus is not bothered by this, however, and rightly so, since this is after all the only case where there is a nature without a corresponding human person.

The remainder of this discussion, which takes place in the replies to the objections, is extremely technical and need not concern us in detail, since Scotus himself evidently did not consider it very important. "Perhaps," he ventures in his concluding paragraph, "this is the real answer—neither as man nor as God is [Jesus] predestined to be the Son of God." What is important, whether or not it constitutes predestination in anyone's rigorous definition  according to which predestination must apply to persons, is that the Lord's humanity *was* from all eternity *meant* to attain eternal and glorious life.

The second of two "doubts" or obscurities that Scotus thought needed clarification is similarly more of a technicality than a real issue. "Which did God intend first, the union of this nature with the Word, or its ordination to glory?" Scotus replies that the end is always willed first, though it is realized last; so in this case glory is the main point, and its means of attainment is, concretely, the re-demptive Incarnation involving the human nature's union with the Word.

Interestingly, it is the first "doubt," rather than the question itself or any of the positions taken pro and con, that contains the real issue around which the entire Scotistic school of Christology has been built and because of which it has borne such rich fruit. The subject of this "doubt" that needs clarification appears, at first sight, to be the same as that expressed by St. Thomas's main question: Would God have become incarnate if man had not sinned? In Scotus's hands, however, the question undergoes a complete transformation. As though accepting Aquinas's admission that we cannot know what *might* have happened *if* things had been otherwise, Scotus ignores that hypo-thetical question totally. "Does this predestination [of Jesus] depend necessarily upon the fall of human nature?" he asks.

His reply is a model of logical clarity:

> One who wills ordinately, and not inordinately, first intends what is nearer the end, and just as he first intends one to have glory before grace, so among those to whom he has foreordained glory, he who wills ordinately would seem to intend first the glory of the one he wishes to be nearest the end, and therefore he intends glory for [Christ] before . . . any other soul, and to every other soul he wills glory before taking into account the opposite

—i.e., anyone's sin or damnation; and thus "No one . . . is predestined simply because God foresaw another would fall, lest anyone have reason to rejoice at the misfortune of another."

Notice how closely this exposition corresponds to the general account we gave in the preceding chapter of pre-destination, according to which it (1) is a divine act of will as well as of knowledge, (2) decrees eternal life for a particular individual, (3) is, as the act of the supremely intelligent Agent, well ordered, and (4) includes the element of "predefinition": God's specific, direct, and immediate decision that specific acts will be performed by the human individual predestined (in this case, the redemptive Incarnation).

God, then, the supremely intelligent Agent, first wills the end, then those nearest the end, and then those further removed from it. This corresponds to the "moments" of our earlier discussion. Ends come first, means second—not in the sense that God works temporally, but in the sense that the end is what counts most, and our way of expressing the end-means relationship in God's plan is metaphorically temporal.

Notice, as a second observation on Scotus's treatment, two specifications of this "ends-before-means" principle: (1) for any individual, glory—attained *later*—is decreed "before" grace, granted *earlier*; and (2) among the realities or events predestined in the comprehensive divine creative plan, it is not Adam, the first man in time, but Jesus, the head of creation summing all things up in himself, who is willed *first*. The Incarnation does not depend on Adam's sin, therefore, and it is not primarily for our redemption that the Word has become flesh.

Thirdly, and—I admit—implicitly: God from eternity "predefined" the mission of Christ, the redemptive Incarnation through which he was to reach his goal of eternal glory ("Was it not ordained that the Christ should suffer and so enter into his glory?"—Lk 24:26).

The basically exegetical treatment of the foregoing paragraphs serves to give the reader an idea of what Duns Scotus actually thought about the role of Jesus in the divine plan for creation, but the predestination of Christ, with which Scotus's main question was concerned, has been subsumed by the Franciscan theologian Jean-F. Bonnefoy (1897-1958) into a fuller systematic synthesis.[13]  The larger context is known as the "Absolute Primacy of Christ." Drawing upon the biblical, patristic, and speculative work done by countless predecessors, as well as upon his own efforts, Bonnefoy has forged an admirably structured perspective which we want to present at this point to cast additional light on what has already been said about Christ's predestination.

The subject at hand, it will be recalled, is the relation of the incarnate Word as such to all the other elements in the divine creative plan. To begin with, then, we have to attend to the possible ways in which anything can be related to anything else. Most obvious—because most superficial and least important—are spatial and temporal relationships. One reality is above, behind, alongside another; or one succeeds or precedes another. Obvious, yes; but, as we also said, trivial. Juxtaposition in space and time implies no important influence, meaning, or personally significant relationship between two entities.

As the Greek philosophers Plato and Aristotle, together with their medieval followers, so clearly saw, influence— mutual interaction and relation—is best expressed in terms of *causality*, which is simply any positive way of entering into the constitution of something else. They distinguished "intrinsic" from "extrinsic" casuality, meaning by the former the internal constituent principles of matter (what something is made out of) and form (what its own inner nature is). These intrinsic causes are of no interest to us here because we are dealing with relationships between two or more realities, not the internal makeup of a single entity.

For Aristotle, the two important extrinsic causes were the efficient cause—the agent who produces another reality and is thus related to it as what we today would call simply its "cause" or "maker"—and the final cause—the end, purpose, or goal governing the production and existence of the reality produced. For Plato, however, a third type of extrinsic cause was even more important than these two: viz., the model or exemplar after which a reality is patterned. In Plato's well known emphasis on transcendence, it was much more imortant to know about the higher realm of reality mirrored in the lower than to dawdle over an analysis of the lower. From the analysis done by the two Greek philosphers, at any rate, we derive a threefold extrinsic causality that can tell us a good deal about the relationships existing between two entities on different levels of reality.

We begin with efficient causality, the influence that a maker or agent—a doer—has upon what he makes, produces, actively influences. Since our concern here is not strictly philosophical, we can deal with efficient causality in a general and brief fashion before determining what it can tell us about the Lord Jesus and his relationship to us and to all other creatures.

As we have said, the efficient cause is an agent who does something; in the simplest terms, the producer of something else called the effect. The cobbler is thus the efficient cause of the shoe, as the parents are of the child. And in the most sublime and profound sense, set forth at the beginning of our first chapter, almighty God himself is the "first" Cause of the entire universe.

Jesus Christ is, of course, God. As eternal Word, God from God and Light from Light, he is co-equal with the Father and the Spirit and hence the first efficient Cause of each one of us and of our whole world. But this is not the point here. In a slow and rather painstaking, step-by-step procedure we are trying to explain, not God's relation to the world, but the relation of Jesus Christ, precisely in his humanity, to every other creature. Is there any sense in which we can say that his human nature is the "efficient cause" of—the "maker" of, the agent who produces—every other creature?

Even among Scotistic theologians down through the ages, there has been a marked reluctance to include this relation of efficient causality in the framework of the Lord's absolute primacy and predestination. Here Bonnefoy stands practically alone in his insistence that to elaborate adequately and completely the relation in question, we must include this most basic type of causality even though it seems difficult at first sight to do so. How can Jesus Christ, in his human nature which came into existence at a definite historical moment some two millenia ago, be said to have caused, not only other creatures after himself (a contention apparently belied by the facts), but even all those who preceded him (an apparent impossiblity)?

Since it cannot be a question, where the Lord's humanity is concerned, of primary efficient causality—actually being the infinite power creating all things from nothing—we must examine *secondary* causality and see whether there is a type of such influence that might apply to Jesus in his humanity. Secondary causality is generally understood as *instrumental*; such is the influence of the tool in the hand of the carpenter. But God can hardly be said to have used his Son's human nature as an instrument the way the builder uses a screwdriver! Bonnefoy therefore suggests the notion of *meritorious* causality, according to which the actions performed by Jesus during his earthly life, especially his passion, death, and resurrection—those crucial, "pre-defined" meritorious acts—would as it were serve as the motive for God to produce everything else that ever existed, exists, or will exist.

This solution is not so contrived as it may first appear to be. It is not a question of having to go in the fashion of a scientist to some empirical situation, examine what presents itself to our senses, and record the data in quantitative form. On the contrary, we are dealing, in this strictly theological context, with an *a priori* norm: Christ is first—uppermost—in God's plan, and what is first bears a strictly causal relationship to what comes after it, lies below it, in any order. Jesus was predestined absolutely to glory, and other realities only for his sake. What he did, his concrete, predefined actions, were his pathway to glory; and those same actions therefore merited not merely his own glory but everything else as well in a world made for him.

The second type of causality mentioned above is that of the end or goal, final causality. The final cause is the reason why the agent acts at all. If I decide to copy a tape recording for a friend, I have to have a *reason*; I can hardly be said just automatically and mechanically to sit down and compulsively turn on the tape deck! My friend himself, my concern for his enjoyment and pleasure, my esteem for his musical taste—all these things enter into the picture and motivate me to copy the tape; they are the final cause of the copy I make.

As the triune Godhead is the primary efficient cause of the universe, so God also is its final cause. In Augustine's immortal phrase, God has made us for himself, and our hearts are restless until they rest in him. It is inconceivable that there be any reality outside or above God which would determine him, motivate him in his perfect self-sufficiency to produce a world of which he has no need.

But again, we are concerned here with secondary causality; and after what has been said so far, we shall surely not find it difficult to understand that the Lord's humanity, first predestined among all creatures to glory, is the secondary end, goal, reason for being, of all the others. Even if we lacked this clear direct insight into the reality involved, we have the Apostle's explicit testimony to the order of final causality that characterizes the divine plan: ". . . the world, life and death, the present and the future, are all your servants; but you belong to Christ and Christ belongs to God" (1 Cor 3:23).

Finally, there is exemplary causality. The exemplar or model is the more perfect reality; the copy, the less perfect. This quintessentially Platonic insight must, of course, be understood in a metaphysical sense. That is, it is meant to apply among levels of natural beings—to characterize the order of nature and not (at least not necessarily) artificial aesthetic products where varying human talent comes into play and the artist may produce a painting which transfigures, actually enhances, the reality he has copied.

For the third time now, we must for completeness include reference to God as primary cause—this time, as primary exemplar. The well known Platonic-Augustinian notion of the divine Ideas was meant to express this facet of the divine creative act. According to Plato, the multiple and imperfect individuals of a species bespeak a unitary and perfect model of which they are mere copies. Augustine transformed this Platonic teaching (which in its original form gave no account of the ontological status of the Ideas—what they actually are or where they are to be "situated") by specifying that the transcendent models or Ideas were actually "ideas" in the mind of the personal Creator, who of course did not figure in Plato's philosophy at all. By these "ideas," Augustine did not mean to introduce real multiplicity into the divine nature; rather, he chose this convenient human way to state the fact that God knows himself in an eternal, unitary, infinite act as imitable in various ways. When he actually produces creatures with a specific nature, we say that he has an "idea" of that nature which is normative for it: is its perfect model or exemplar which it, as a finite creature, can only approximate but never perfectly represent.

In what sense can Jesus be said, in his humanity, to be the model or exemplary cause of every other creature—to exercise at his own "secondary" or created level a uniquely full participation in the exemplary causality which is fully and infinitely his as Word of God? We must realize that it is not a question of examining his humanity empirically—to seek as it were a blueprint for every other created reality— the redness of the rose, the height of the pyramids, or the brittleness of a piece of bone china! As it has been through- out this discussion of the Lord's causal relationship to the rest of creation, so now our perspective is transempirical— metaphysical.

A reflective metaphysics deals, not in empirical par- ticulars, but in essential perfections—universal structures that characterize the various levels of being. What are these levels? From the most modest chemical element of hydro- gen, up through the increasing complexities of vegetative, sentient, and spiritual life with its created reflection of divine intelligence and love, we are able to conceive a synthetic hierarchy of "grades of being" that we see present in the humanity of Jesus in an unparalleled way. We see, e.g., in the very materiality of his body, now permeated with the glory of divine life to which he was from the first as man predestined, the paradigm of all material creation. We see exemplified in him, with a harmony found nowhere else, life in its fullness. Whatever there is of goodness, of perfection, of beauty, of existential reality, is summed up in an unparalleled way in him, in whom are found all the treasures of wisdom and knowledge, the fullness of beauty and love.

One may of course wonder whether materiality, with the vulnerability, corruptibility, and multiplicity it involves, precludes our identifying the Lord's humanity as the apex of created perfection. His soul, maybe; but his entire human nature? And even his soul—essentially linked to and even weighed down by the materiality of his body? The angels, after all, are pure spirits, not burdened with matter at all and so more perfectly unified and able to live the life of the spirit with an ardor unimpeded by matter and its demands. Yes—theoretically and prescinding from the mystery of the Incarnation, there is a good deal of truth to the Platonic insight that unity and being are equivalent and that there is therefore a certain degradation involved in that dispersion into multiplicity which is matter.

But—and this is one of Teilhard's most notable contributions—with the Incarnation matter itself becomes transformed. Its meaning and value are to be discerned, no longer through the categories of an abstract metaphysics, but rather in light of the fact that the eternal, divine Word has acted, continues to act, and will forever act in and through a material, chemical, biological, sensory human body that is *his own*. Pope St. Leo the Great caught something of the stunning paradox involved here in his first sermon on the Ascension:

> [The Apostles] had a great and inexpressible cause for joy when [they] saw man's nature rising above the dignity of the whole heavenly creation, above the ranks of angels, above the exalted status of archangels. Nor would there be any limit to its upward course until humanity was admitted to a seat at the right hand of the eternal Father, to be enthroned at last in the glory of him to whose nature it was wedded in the person of the Son.[14]

Jesus gives meaning to the universe—not only to human life, but literally to everything else that exists in this universe of ours. There is no level of being which he does not in an eminent way embody in himself, including the intensely vibrant life of the angels. Plausible as it may have seemed at first to speculate on the superiority of their purely spiritual life over his "mixed," human life, further reflection has thus led us to conclude that precisely because of the hypostatic union—the union of his soul and body to the divinity in the single Person of the Word—such abstract speculations are out of order. His dignity derives from his Person, the dignity of his humanity derives directly from its union with his divinity, and that humanity essentially includes bodiliness.

Our brief exposition of Duns Scotus's treatment of our Lord's predestination contained the essential point: that of the "absoluteness" of the divine predestining act, its quality of being unconditioned by any other consideration, any other creature or historical event. We need not, then, repeat here all that was said in that context. All we need do is mention that the threefold causality of Jesus relative to all other creatures, the causal influence we have been examining in the foregoing paragraphs, is the concrete, active manifestation and implemenation of what God intended, *predestined*, for his incarnate Son from all eternity. That causal relationship is, therefore, explained by and presupposes the predestining decree providing for it, and Jesus is rightly said to be predestined in the "first moment" of God's creative plan.

Finally, according to Bonnefoy's synthesis, both the causal priority and the priority of the predestination are subsumed under the most general notion of all, that of the absolute and universal "primacy" of Jesus Christ—of the incarnate Word precisely *as* incarnate. In his specific causal relationship to all other creatures, then, as well as in the absolute character of his own predestination, Jesus Christ is clearly shown, in the majestically striking phrase of the Apostle Paul, to be "first in every way" (Col 1:18).

This third chapter has formed a transition, as it were, from our initial general considerations on creation and predestination to the ensuing explanation of the predestination and Immaculate Conception of the Blessed Virgin Mary. The transition is clearly required because of the intimate link between Mary's role in God's plan and that of her Son.

It was essential, to begin with, that we have a correct understanding of the Incarnation itself as the joining, without fusion or modification of either, of humanity and divinity in the abiding, eternal Person of the divine Word. Any conceptual framework that is unable to provide an account of this sublime reality is incompatible with orthodox Catholic teaching on the Incarnation.

In the second place, we examined the reasoning of John Duns Scotus, according to which the humanity of Jesus in virtue of its hypostatic union with the divinity was "absolutely" predestined to glory: predestined, that is, independently of original sin and the consequent need for redemption.

Finally, we considered the systematic elaboration of the doctrine of our Lord's "absolute primacy" by Jean-F. Bonnefoy, in which the literal "first place" implies predestination in the "first moment" of the divine creative plan, which in turn implies a secondary but universal causal influence with respect to every other creature.

*Chapter IV*
*The Blessed Virgin Mary*
*in God's Plan*

# Chapter IV

# THE BLESSED VIRGIN MARY
# IN GOD'S PLAN

THE UNIQUELY INTIMATE LINK between the pre-destination of Jesus Christ as Head of creation and that of the Blessed Virgin Mary to be his Mother has already been referred to several times. The eternal decree in virtue of which God determined to take to himself a human nature immediately implies his selection of a human Mother. It also implies his "predefining" of the singularly blessed, virtuous, and fruitful life of the Woman he chose.

It is hardly surprising, therefore, that our Lady's pre-destination takes on a singular importance in such systematic presentations of Mariology as the manual tract of Joseph A. de Aldama and the *Twentieth-Century Encyclopedia of Catholicism* volume by Cardinal Suenens.[1] In fact, both these monographs open with a discussion of Mary's predestination, de Aldama's explicitly, and Suenens's implicitly under the title "Mary in the Divine Plan." Appearances, however, can be deceptive. Let us examine these two representative treatments.

De Aldama's "Mariology" opens with a four-page "chapter" entitled "On the Predestination of Mary to be the Mother of the Redeemer." In fact, he never speaks of "predestination" at all but rather of our Lady's "election," and his concern, expressed in the customary manual form of a thesis, is to establish that our Lady's choice as Mother of the Redeemer was gratuitous on God's part. His argument is of course wholly cogent, but the narrow scope of its vision is disappointing inasmuch as it contains no trace of the breathtaking Pauline vista of a universe made to be the everlasting kingdom of Jesus Christ and his Blessed Mother. Mary's election is a free act on God's part, yes; but how is it related to the predestination of the other elect? What is her rightful place in the overall divine plan for creation? All we learn from this treatment is that she "pertains to the soteriological order and to the hypostatic order," but no conclusion is drawn from this pregnant observation.[2]

Cardinal Suenens opens his discussion with slightly better promise: "In order to understand [Mary], we must go back in thought to the beginning of the world, to God's creative mind. In the last analysis, why did God create the world?" In limpid prose and with keen insight, the author replies with Paul: "For Christ."

> He it is, indeed, who is the beginning and the end, the last word on everything. In him creation holds together, he is the keystone of the arch, the supreme why and wherefore. Everything, heaven and earth, things visible and invisible, history, space, all has been made in view of our Lord Jesus Christ.[3]

And the Mariological implication is duly drawn: "But if the Incarnation lies at the heart of God's creative action, it is Mary who makes that Incarnation possible, and therein lies her incomparable greatness."

What bright promise! But it is short-lived. Only a few lines later we read, "The mysterious origin of the Blessed Virgin . . . was foreseen and ordained by one and the same decree with the Incarnation . . . . It *might* even *possibly* exist independently of the redemption of the world."[4] After a paragraph's discussion of the Thomistic and Scotistic conceptions of the divine plan, the author says, "Whether or not this [the absolute predestination of Jesus and Mary] may be, even if in God the decision of the Incarnation was subsequent to original sin," everything still converges toward Mary "just as by its attraction the sea controls the course of the rivers."

Beautiful image; but the strength of its foundation has been sapped. If "this" may *not* be, then neither may "that." Unless Mary's predestination is absolute, things cannot converge toward her. ". . . one who wills ordinately, and not inordinately, first intends what is nearer the end, and so . . . He who wills ordinately, would seem to intend first the glory of the one He wishes to be nearest the end . . . ."[5]

Of course Cardinal Suenens is exquisitely correct: "just as by its attraction the sea controls the course of the rivers," so things do in fact converge toward Jesus and Mary. This is the major contention of the present chapter. Our main point is precisely that just as the decree for the Incarnation itself does not "break in" upon a universe originally created with no provision for it, so neither is our Lady's role an "afterthought" in God's mind, contigent on original sin and the need for redemption from it.

To put it in slightly different terms, we want to lay to rest any suspicion that the predestination of the Blessed Virgin is something "wholly other," unrelated to the original, primal divine creative plan. We want to present a framework in which it is impossible to have an isolated Mariology unrelated to all the rest of theology and human knowledge; in which it is impossible to have a Marian devotion closed in on itself—a "me-and-Mary" spirituality akin to the "me-and-God" religiosity that many people were alleged by the avant-garde theologians of the 1950s and 60s to have indulged in before Vatican II. Like that of Jesus, Mary's role is cosmic, crucial to the world's being and history, absolute and universal.

Her predestination, then, is not something to be looked at as an isolated action on God's part, much less as an afterthought, conceived by God "after"—in dependence upon—Adam's sin and the need for redemption. Rather it is, after the Incarnation, the most important, central, crucial element in the whole creative plan.

"After" the Incarnation itself, we have just said. Can the selection of his Mother really be said to be "after" the Lord's decision to become man? Not, obviously, in any sense which would literally imply temporal succession in the divine decree itself—a matter already discussed in the preceding chapters. But there is a more important sense in which the selection of Mary to be the Mother of the Incarnate Word cannot be said to be "after" the decree for the Incarnation itself. That is, it cannot be a separate decree at all from the one determining the Word's Incarnation, even in the mitigated sense in which other "moments" of the creative plan are distinct. Hence the expression of Pope Pius IX in the Bull *Ineffabilis Deus*, defining the Immaculate Conception: "one and the same decree" (*uno eodemque decreto*). There is a greater distinction, e.g., between the decisions to create angels and to create a material universe than there is between the decision to become incarnate and the selection of a human Mother for the Word.

Once again, even at the risk of undue repetition, it may be helpful to emphasize that the distinctions we human beings make as we try to analyze God's creative plan are not intended to be projected into the very being of the divine mind and will. Rather, they are based on our experience of the various causal relationships between creatures or on knowledge of those relationships communicated to us in divine revelation. The knowledge and will of God are a simple unity, but a unity of richness rather than poverty. The multiplicity and order that become explicit in creation itself thus have a real basis, a real foundation in the rich and simple unity of God's single, infinitely fecund and unified plan.

This is why we can say that even in God's eternal creative decree there is a *closer* union between the Incarnation and our Lady's predestination than there is between the angels and material creation. Being human means having a mother; the implication is so tight that the Blessed Virgin joins her Son on the unique level of being which we have seen Father de Aldama correctly identify as the "hypostatic order." This is an order not separated from or remote from, but firmly embedded in, the creative plan at its apex, its peak, its zenith. It is called "hypostatic" because it comprises the union of the divine and the human in one "hypostasis" or Person. And Mary is the mother of that Person, the eternal Word of God.

To understand our Lady's predestination, then, we need not construct a whole new framework. We need only apply to her, as we have done in the case of her Son, the general principles governing the analysis of predestination itself. That is, we must begin by affirming that God in sovereign freedom predestined her first of all to glory—to eternal life in intimate union with her Creator. This, being the "end," is the first "moment" of her predestination.

Next, we recall that predestination to eternal life implies provision of the means to attain that life: graces and merits. The graces are bestowed by God so that the free creature can earn his destiny through the merits—i.e., by fulfilling the mission entrusted to him and by persevering in the Lord's service. In our Lady's case it is not a matter of some modicum of sanctifying grace, but rather the unparalleled fullness of grace from the very first moment of her existence which we call the Immaculate Conception, and from that moment on there continued to flood upon her grace upon grace, blessing upon blessing. As regards merits or cooperation with those graces, we may say in a similar vein that in Mary's case it is hardly a matter of the off-again, on-again cooperation found in the lives of other human beings, but rather the supreme docility which gave her a unique role with her Son in our redemption and entitles her to be called Coredemptrix.

And finally, we repeat the important point that each and every action of the free creature is "predefined" by God: all his good actions are intended by God directly and immediately as conducive to his destiny. This does not imply determinism, as we have seen—at least for the Congruist school—but it does imply a profound mystery. God does choose the actions, intend them, set things up for the creature to perform them; and yet the creature freely assents to what God proposes. The act truly belongs both to God and to the creature—wholly and not partly to each, but in different ways. But if predestination always includes all the meritorious actions of a person's life, then in our Lady's case we have to look to the entire mystery of her life to understand her predestination adequately. Her unique role in God's creative plan is of course fundamental, but no detail of her life is irrelevant to an appreciation of our subject. Her childhood marked by complete cooperation with God's Law and will as it became manifest to her, her consent to Gabriel's invitation, her intimate life with her Son as she brought him to manhood, her cooperation in his redemptive act, and the role she has assumed as spiritual mother and privileged intercessor for all of human-kind: all of these are rich sources of information on the meaning of Mary's predestination.

Some years ago, when manuals, textbooks, and mono-graphs on Mariology as a distinct branch of theology began to proliferate, their authors disagreed on what they called the "primary principle" of their science. What, they asked, is the most fundamental thing that can be said of our Lady? Some of them suggested a single such principle, such as her divine motherhood, her status as the new Eve, as type of the Church, or as the human person most perfectly redeemed. Others sought a more complex but still unified characterization of the fundamental privilege with which Mary has been endowed: "Mother-Coredemptrix," "Mother-Spouse," etc. And still others thought they had discovered two co-equal principles: Mother of God and spiritual mother of mankind, or Mother of God and Coredemptrix.

Today, in our less scholastic atmosphere, many of us are somewhat less interested in the elaboration of strictly argued theses and scientific structures than were those earlier theologians. But it is difficult to justify abandoning some needed minimum of orderly and reflective analysis, of logically structured synthesis. To do that would be to abandon the theological enterprise itself and to be content with an exclusively devotional or inspirational approach devoid of the unified perspective which speculative theology alone can provide.

The question of the "fundamental principle of Mariology" thus remains an important one. It is of importance in our context because its answer tells us precisely to what our Lady was primarily predestined. The reader will have

noticed in the representative list above the prevalence of
"Mother of God" among the privileges suggested as primary. Nevertheless, our choice is not made on the basis of
numerical popularity. Not merely because a majority of
theologians have specified our Lady's divine motherhood
as the basis for all other privileges she enjoys, but more
importantly because of the logical requirements of all that
has been said about the divine plan and Mary's role in it,
we maintain that her predestination to be the Mother of
Jesus Christ is absolutely fundamental—the single factor
that explains everything else about her.[6]

Many theologians have been able to say precisely that—
that the divine motherhood underlies the whole mystery
of Mary—even in the perspective generally referred to as
Thomistic. That is, even in an outlook in which the Incarnation depends upon original sin and is therefore seen as an
"afterthought," an "amendment" to the original creative
plan, those theologians have maintained that once there *is*
provision for the Incarnation, it is precisely the part that
Mary plays in the Incarnation, as the Mother of Jesus, that
renders her singularly blessed and sets her apart in the
hypostatic order.

But in the Scotistic perspective of the Absolute Primacy
of Jesus Christ, it is still easier to see the reason for Mary's
quite special dignity. Sin and redemption remain very
much a part of the picture, of course.[7] But they are secondary in the sense that they do not determine the very
existence of the hypostatic order itself. Rather, just as the
Lord's predestination is absolute—unconditioned by any
other reality—so is that of his Blessed Mother. This same
Scotistic perspective adds a striking clarity and cogency,
moreover, to the various methodological principles that
Mariologists have used: the principles of transcendence,
of fittingness, of eminence, of analogy, and of association.

Illustrations of this contention will be given in the ensuing paragraphs.

When we completed the mainly exegetical discussion of Scotus's question on the absolute predestination of Jesus in the preceding chapter, we felt that it would not entail undue repetition to sum up and systematize what had been said in the synthesis suggested by Jean-F. Bonnefoy. In the same way here, it seems that additional coherence and understanding can be attained by the use of that same synthesis, including the notion of "primacy" that expresses literally the status of the Blessed Virgin in the universe created by God, that of predestination to that status, and that of a threefold causal influence with respect to all other creatures.

Jesus Christ, we have said, enjoys an absolute and universal primacy in the created order. He is, in his human nature, the "first creature" to be conceived in God's creative plan, and his headship means that the whole universe is created with him in mind—that it all makes sense only because of him. Now, in virtue of what Mariologists call the "principle of analogy," we are able to say something similar of the Blessed Virgin. This principle states that whatever is said of Jesus is to be asserted, not exactly in the same manner or to the same degree, but still positively and literally, of his Mother. So closely conjoined is her role with his, that she is said, not in any adventitious or whimsical way, but literally and in a richly meaningful sense, to be Queen of the Universe. It is not merely licit, not merely useful, but necessary to speak of the Blessed Virgin's "absolute primacy," subordinate to but intimately linked with that of her Son, over every other creature.

When we discussed our Lord's primacy in the preceding chapter, we did not feel constrained to address the implication of *power* in the term because most Christians are comfortable enough with the doctrine of Jesus as Judge and King. Perhaps, though, they are too comfortable with it and are willing to be content with the image of Jesus as "Pantokrator" so familiar in the icons of the Eastern Church. (Those unfamiliar with the depths of oriental theology and art often feel that the icons depict Jesus as sternly fixing the hapless lambs and goats with an icy stare.[8]) Jesus does, of course, have from the hands of his Father "all authority in heaven and on earth" (Mt 28:18); but his is not an arbitrary, despotic authority, not that of the "pagans" among whom the rulers "lord it" over them and the "great men make their authority felt" (Mt 20:25). It is that of the Son of Man [who] came not to be served but to serve" (Mt 20:28). The real Lord does not need to *play* Lord or to "lord it"; his dignity shines forth from his inmost being in the form of loving solicitude for his brothers and sisters, and if there is any judging or condemning to be done, he does not do it with a vindictive relish.

Similarly, it would be a deplorable distortion to regard our Blessed Mother's Queenship as that of Elizabeth I writ large. Like that of Jesus, her regal dignity shines forth from her maternal heart in the form of devoted concern for all of us who have been entrusted to her care. Her absolute and universal primacy is, let us repeat it, that of a tender and loving mother; she does, without doubt, occupy that central and exalted position denoted by "primacy." Everything does, in Cardinal Suenens's beautiful image, converge toward her as rivers toward the sea. But her influence, her power, her queenship consist, not in repressing all else, but in exalting it.

The second element in Bonnefoy's synthesis is the Lord's absolute *predestination*. Not only was Jesus said to enjoy *in fact* the primacy or first place in creation; not only was he said to have been granted it, not as a sort of after-thought or because of some action he happened to have performed without its being predefined in God's eternal plan; but he was said to have been absolutely and unconditionally predestined from all eternity to occupy that primacy. In virtue of the same principle of analogy, as we saw in the opening pages of this chapter, the same thing must be said of our Lady because of her role as Mother of the Incarnate Word. She too is literally and properly said to be absolutely, unconditionally predestined to share in her Son's primacy. This gives full weight to the second methodological principle of Mariology to be brought into play here, that of "singularity" or "transcendence," according to which there are properly attributed to our Lady unique privileges not appropriate to other creatures. The privileges flow immediately from the priority of her predestination; that is to say, they correspond to the predefined actions that constitute her own path to glory. One thinks immediately, here, of her Immaculate Conception once again, of her freedom from any actual sin and from concupiscence, and of the unique degree of her participation in her Son's redemptive act.

What of the threefold causality that Jesus was said to exercise with respect to the rest of creation? It will be recalled that his relation to other creatures was discussed in terms of efficient (meritorious) causality, final causality, and exemplary causality. We know that, since these modes of influence flow from the position a person's predestination occupies in God's creative plan, the Blessed Virgin must exercise them vis-à-vis every creature "after" or "below" her in the universe.

Consider meritorious causality first, according to which Jesus, by every pure, virtuous, loving act he performed during his entire lifetime on earth, merited not merely humankind's redemption, but the very creation of the universe. Surely it is not difficult to see that the principle of analogy applies once again here, as it does through all of Mariology. The Blessed Virgin's purity, virtue, and love were superior to those of every other creature, were as perfect as a creature's could be and hence "second" (if we may put it thus) only to those of her divine Son. If his life could be said to be meritorious, then surely in its own way and to its own degree, so can hers.

But it was in his paschal journey through suffering and death to new and risen life that the Lord showed forth the fullness and perfection of his love, the love greater than which no human being can show (Jn 15:13). Similarly it is to Calvary that we must look for the fullest expression of his Mother's love. As Simeon's prophecy came to its realization and that sword of grief pierced Mary's motherly heart (Lk 2:35), we know that she suffered in her inmost soul all that Jesus suffered in his body. This is why she has been accorded the title of Coredemptrix: her sufferings were in their own way and to their own degree redemptive for humankind and the fallen universe.[8] This title drew a good deal of criticism when it was popularized some years ago, especially in Protestant circles where it was interpreted as derogating from the role of Jesus as unique Mediator between God and human beings and sole Redeemer of the human race (cf. 1 Tim 2:5). The criticism was, however, unfortunate and misguided. Still another of the Mariological principles mentioned earlier is helpful in dispelling it: that of "association." Predestined to be the Lord's Mother, Mary was by that very fact called to be his associate, his closest collaborator, in his redemptive mission. It is not as though her life, her purity, her virtue, her suffering had to be taken in isolation as independently sufficient for our redemption, or had in some way to be pitted against those of her Son. That would be a truly grotesque distortion of the whole perspective presented in the foregoing pages. Participation, not competition, is the proper concept here. If the Blessed Virgin's role is thus properly understood, however, she is clearly seen to be, in a subordinate and participatory way, the universal meritorious cause, together with her Son, not only of mankind's redemption, but of the very existence of every creature outside the hypostatic order.

As Jesus is the final as well as meritorious cause—the very reason for being—of every other creature, so too his Mother shares in that universal finality. It may be worth recalling that there is no intention, in this systematic synthesis, of separating the elements of God's creative plan. We do not imply any dissociation of its "moments," parts, or levels. We are not theorizing about some hypothetical universe which would consist, say, of only Jesus, Mary, and angels. God is not being said to have conceived the hypostatic order in one act and then to have been struck by the fittingness of making a human race to complement the existence of the Incarnate Word and his Mother. The divine creative plan is a seamless unity, and our task is only to discern the intrinsic relationships that link its various elements. In this unified perspective, it is most appropriate to say that the subordinate element "exists for" the more perfect. And so it is accurate, and it aids our understanding and appreciation of our Blessed Mother, to specify that she is the universal final cause of all creatures outside the hypostatic order, in the sense that she participates in a subordinate but true and literal way in her Son's role as the world's end and goal.

Finally, there is the causal influence of the model or exemplar. Jesus, we have said, is in his humanity the secondary but universal exemplary cause of every other creature. As we should expect, his Mother shares in this role also. In the striking phrase of St. Albert the Great, "whatever a mere creature can receive, who is receptive to God, all this was communicated to the Lord's Mother."[9]

Here we see operative the final Mariological principle to be brought into play in our synthesis: that of "eminence," according to which God has bestowed upon Mary in some way—whether as such in a better way, or in an equivalent way—all the privileges that he has given to any of his saints. But our perspective of her absolute primacy in creation enables us to go beyond the customary narrow interpretation that restricts the principle to "all the privileges that [God] has given to any of his *saints.*"[10] While agreeing that the supernatural order, the realm of grace, is of primary importance and that nature is itself as a whole ordered to grace, we should also realize that grace does not on that account eliminate or destroy nature. The absolute primacy, unconditioned predestination, and threefold causal influence of Jesus and Mary extends, therefore, to the realm of nature too. We thus interpret the principle of eminence to apply, not only to the privileges that God has given to his saints in the order of supernatural merit and grace, but (just as in the case of her Son) to the whole hierarchy of perfections that constitutes the natural order. The treasures of wisdom and knowledge, the beauty of unsullied human nature that recapitulate the universe in Jesus do so likewise in a subordinate and participatory way in Mary, his Mother.

Father René Laurentin provides in a fine and challenging article the sort of application to concrete human life to which the doctrine of Mary's exemplarity lends itself.[11] Defending the doctrine against objections based on a crudely empirical interpretation, he shows that our Lady is an "intensive," theological model and not an "extensive," empirical one. It will not do, therefore, in opposition to our position, to point out that our Lady cannot be a model for males because she is female; Jesus himself, Father Laurentin points out, is a model, not only for males but for human beings as such; and this is just as true of his Mother.

Again, it is myopic to say that because the Blessed Virgin did not know the solitude of the cloister, she cannot be a model for nuns; that because she did not know sensuality, she cannot be a model for wives; that because she did not know the scattering of her affections among several children, she cannot be a model for mothers. As the Evangelical Anglican writer John de Satgé has so clearly grasped, our Lady is indeed the "prototype of the whole human race,"[12] including males, nuns, wives, and mothers. She is the new Eve, Mother of all the living, prototype, in her docility to God's word and solicitude to accomplish his will, of the Church and of all humankind as both ideally should be.

Thus does the systematic synthesis of Bonnefoy shed light on the absolute predestination of the Blessed Virgin Mary. In the perspective of that synthesis we see her predestination to glory to be specified in the modality of a motherly role. Our Lady is unconditionally, eternally predestined to the hypostatic order, and in virtue of the dignity which is hers as Mother of creation's Head and King, she is responsible with him for leading all things to their fulfillment according to the divine creative plan.

*Chapter V*
*The Immaculate Conception*

# Chapter V

# THE IMMACULATE CONCEPTION

IN DISCUSSING our Lady's predestination in the preceding chapter, we mentioned in passing several of her privileges or roles in the creative plan, including that of being mankind's spiritual Mother, Coredemptrix, Queen of the Universe, and type of the Church. All these, we said, flow naturally from her primary role as Mother of the Incarnate Word; and all these will have to be explored in subsequent volumes of the present series.

But there is one privilege in particular that we consider fitting to treat in this volume both for systematic and for historical reasons. That is her Immmaculate Conception. Systematically: we hope to show that the Immaculate Conception is fully and consistently intelligible only in the perspective of the systematic synthesis we used in the two preceding chapters. Historically: as a matter of fact, the theologians who defended Mary's Immaculate Conception through the stormy debates of late medieval and modern times were the same ones who espoused the doctrine of her and her Son's absolute primacy and predestination. Theologians who maintained that the Lord's existence as man depended upon sin and the need for redemption consistently maintained that his Mother could not possibly have been conceived without original sin or at least some kind of "debt" or "obligation" to contract it.

That the Blessed Virgin Mary was conceived without any stain of sin was solemnly defined in 1854 by Pope Pius IX in these words:

> We declare, pronounce, and define that the Most Blessed Virgin Mary, at the first instant of her Conception was preserved immaculate from all stain of original sin, by the singular grace and privilege of the Omnipotent God, in virtue of the merits of Jesus Christ, the Savior of mankind, and that this doctrine was revealed by God, and therefore, must be believed firmly and constantly by all the faithful.[1]

Why a solemn definition in 1854? The year seems rather late. If our Lady's Immaculate Conception was supposed to be "believed firmly and constantly by all the faithful," is it possible that it was *not* thus believed for eighteen centuries? One is reminded of the only similar case of a solemn papal definition out of conciliar context, that of our Lady's Assumption, defined by Pope Pius XII almost a century later. Can it be that these Marian doctrines were fabricated by the popes out of whole cloth—that after almost two millennia of Catholic religious life and belief two quite new, as yet unheard of, doctrines regarding the Blessed Virgin just sprang up, as it were, out of nowhere?

To restrict our considerations to the topic at hand, the Immaculate Conception, we must reply that this cannot have been the case. Thanks to the unwavering guidance of the Holy Spirit, the faithful had well known all along what to believe. It was the theologians, rather, who had caused such great difficulties as to make a solemn papal definition necessary. This is not to imply a perversity on their part, of course; as we shall see, they had good reason for concern and irreprochable intentions in their opposition to the doctrine. But before we turn to this perplexing situation among theologians and endeavor to explain it, let us proceed with a more positive explanation of the doctrine's basis in revelation, i.e., in sacred Scripture, which has always been regarded as a primary source of revealed doctrine.

Of course not every Catholic teaching can be found explicitly stated in the Bible, but it is helpful to see what possible basis a particular doctrine does have in the sacred text. Again, one cannot naively open the Bible without careful preparation—seize upon a sentence, and assume that because of one's preconceptions and/or the apparently explicit meaning of its words taken out of their context, it serves as proof for one's position. It is rather because of a long tradition, culminating in the authoritative example of Popes Pius IX and Pius XII, that we are led confidently to refer to two such texts: the so-called "Protoevangelium" (literally, "first proclamation of the Good News") in Genesis 3:15; and the Lucan Annunciation narrative (1:28) as implying the Immaculate Conception of the Blessed Virgin Mary.

The former text reads, in the Jerusalem Bible translation, as follows: "I will make you enemies of each other, you and the woman, your offspring and her offspring. It will crush your head and you will strike its heel." God is addressing the serpent and promising a complete, total, absolute opposition between it, symbolizing the Devil, and "the woman." It would be fatuous to pretend that the author of Genesis had an explicit awareness of the doctrine of the Incarnation itself, much less of the Immaculate Conception. Nevertheless, emboldened by a long tradition, many theologians as well as the two modern popes mentioned above have not hesitated to assert that the sentence does indeed apply to Mary, at least in some "eminent" or "fuller" sense of which the human author himself need not have been at all aware. The Holy Spirit has no need, really, for the complete understanding of the human author regarding what he is inspired to write. Nor is it of any real *theological* importance (whatever is to be said of the question from the standpoint of purely *biblical* methodology) whether Mary is implicitly included in "the woman" or "the offspring." The obvious point is the complete opposition or "enmity" between her and the Devil, which later tradition has taken to mean that there can never have been the slightest domination of Mary by Satan (which would be the case if she had been conceived in original sin), nor even any "obligation" to contract original sin, from which obligation she would have been dispensed in a "later" moment of the divine decree that the Word be born of a pure and sinless creature. There is, in other words, no connection whatever between the Blessed Virgin Mary and any kind of sin, original or actual.

According to Luke's Gospel account of the Annunciation, the Archangel Gabriel visited Mary and addressed her in these words (again, in the version of the Jerusalem Bible): "Rejoice, so highly favored! The Lord is with you." In the context, essential for an accurate interpretation, the expression "highly favored" (Greek κεχαριτωμένη, usually translated "full of grace) implies the favor or grace of Mary's divine motherhood. That is, one cannot just excerpt the phrase and speculate about the term's dictionary meaning. Its point is that Mary, about to become the Mother of the incarnate Word, is precisely *thus* filled with grace, "highly favored." The principle of fittingness, which we must now add to the others brought into play in the preceding chapter, is used by theologians to show that the specific way in which Mary was "highly favored," viz., her election to be the Mother of God, implies the absolute opposition already described in our consideration of the Protoevangelium: total freedom from any stain of sin. This interpretation, cogent as it is in itself, also enjoys the weight of authority in that it was set forth by both Pope Pius IX and Pope Pius XII.[2]

As we have mentioned, this interpretation of our Lady's freedom from sin has a long history in the living faith of Christians. In the earliest days of the Church it was, like so many others doctrines, implicit rather than spelled out. It is implicit, for instance, in the widespread patristic use of the Eve-Mary parallel, in which the Blessed Virgin is depicted as canceling out the Devil's destructive attack on the human race. And it is likewise implied in the adjectives used by many of the Fathers to describe Mary: "holy," "innocent," "most pure," "inviolate," and even "immaculate."[3]

The highly influential St. Augustine, however, went on record with an ambivalent teaching. On the one hand, he did clearly acknowledge the common and popular belief that for the sake of God's own honor there could be no question whatever of sin where Mary is concerned. But, on the other hand, so sharp had his ongoing debate with the Pelagians become (and hence so prominent in his thought the need to defend the universality of original sin and the universal need for grace) that he even included our Lady in that universal human condition, adding only this nuance, that she was quickly purified from the universal human condition bound up with conception and birth by a singular grace of rebirth. This obscuring of the earlier, clearly orthodox belief in our Lady's freedom from all stain of sin, resulting from Augustine's struggle against the Pelagians lasted in Western theology until the twelfth century.

Those aware of the intimate connection over the Christian centuries between faith and liturgical celebration do not find it surprising that where theology had gone astray it should be brought back gradually to the truth by the concrete expression of popular faith which is the liturgy. Long before the medieval controversy there had been in the Eastern Churches a devout and enthusiastic celebration of the Feast of our Lady's Immaculate Conception. When the feast was introduced in Europe, however, the theological climate of the eleventh and twelfth centuries caused it to be met with strong opposition, especially on the part of the influential Cistercian Abbot, St. Bernard of Clairvaux (d. 1153). Notwithstanding this opposition, the celebration of the feast spread widely, and with it, naturally, came resurgence of the doctrine's acceptance among theologians. The stage was set for the renowned controversy between the Dominicans following Thomas Aquinas and the Franciscans following John Duns Scotus. Because of Scotus's solution to the various misgivings expressed by so many earlier theologians, and also thanks to the vigorous support of Church authorities, including the Council of Basle (1439) and Pope Sixtus IV (1476/77) the path was clear to the gradual restoration throughout the West of the original, orthodox doctrine of our Lady's Immaculate Conception.

The statement of the doctrine given at this chapter's outset in the words of the papal definition is positive, straightforward, and quite simple. There is no connection—rather there is a complete and absolute opposition—between the Devil and sin on the one hand, and the Blessed Virgin Mary on the other. It ought to be just as straightforward, positive, and simple to explain the teaching; but such, unfortunately, is not the case precisely because of the historical factors just mentioned: Augustine's anti-Pelagian polemic and the pervasive influence it had down through the ages.

For this reason, our own exposition must begin, unfortunately, on a negative note. That is, as we now set out to give a systematic account of the doctrine's meaning, we must first deal with the Augustinian objections to it and counter those objections. Only then will it be possible in a positive way to fulfill the promise made at the beginning of our chapter: to show how the doctrine of the Immaculate Conception flows from the doctrinal synthesis elaborated in Chapters III and IV.

Augustine was correct in insisting on the universality of original sin. As Paul wrote to the Romans, ". . . sin entered the world through one man, and through sin death, and thus death has spread through the whole human race because everyone has sinned" (Rom 5:12). We need not go into the excessively physical interpretation Augustine placed on the doctrine (linking it in no small part, because of his own personal experience as a youth, to the biology of reproduction). But we may be content to agree that he was absolutely right in maintaining that every single human being descended from the first man,[4] being under that man's *moral headship*, derives thereby the stain of original sin. If the Blessed Virgin is a human being among human beings, a member of "Adam's race," then there simply must be some "connection" between her and original sin.

Before the dogma of her Immaculate Conception was defined, it was easy enough to say that she in fact contracted original sin. Then "full of grace" or "highly favored" could be interpreted to mean a cleansing granted to her *after* conception, in view of her destiny to be the Mother of God. Once the dogma was defined, however, this could no longer be said. Those who had said it now turned to a device that even the "immaculists" had long felt constrained to use in order to safeguard the Pauline doctrine on the universality of sin. That is, they postulated, not the actual contraction of original sin and subsequent cleansing, but some kind of "debt" or "obligation" (Latin *debitum*) to contract it. This "debt" assumed various forms.

Some theologians held that our Lady's flesh was actually in some way "infected" up to the moment of its animation by her soul (her conception) so that, were it not for God's timely intervention, it would similarly have "infected" her soul. So crudely physical is this interpretation, however, that such Thomists as Cajetan (Tommaso de Vio, 1469-1534), who were otherwise so attracted to the Augustinian viewpoint, found it repellent.[5]

Others therefore espoused a second theory, that of a "proximate debt" or obligation—moral rather than physical—to contract original sin. According to this viewpoint, Mary was supposed to contract it, but in view of the sublime destiny God had decreed for her as his Mother, he exempted her from that obligation "at a certain predetermined time."[6] Of course they did not mean to imply that God's actions themselves took place in time; rather, as we have explained in discussing predestination, they placed the "moment" of the divine creative and redemptive decree in which Mary was exempted from actually contracting original sin "after" the one in which she was "supposed to" contract it.

Still others, especially after the definition, and ostensibly following the Scotistic view on the creative plan, propose that the Blessed Virgin was not actually *supposed to* contract original sin. Rather, she was "supposed to" be included under Adam's headship, in virtue of which she "would have been supposed to" contract original sin. This is the concept of a "remote," rather than "proximate," obligation to contract original sin—remote, because one step further removed from the actual danger of contracting it, by reason of being exempted from inclusion in Adam's moral headship.

A final refuge has been sought by some, according to which there is no longer said to be any sort of "personal" debt, but rather one of "nature." Virtually no one can make any sense of such a phrase, however,[7] for a reason implicit in our explanation of "person" and "nature" in Chapter III: the nature is only an intrinsic principle of the person's activity. Not being an autonomous reality at all, it cannot be either an agent or a recipient of anything, including sin or obligation.

Movement has, at any rate, been from the earlier toward the later of the above devices, and the logical conclusion is obviously the elimination of any postulated "obligation" or "debt" whatever. How this can be done, and the Pauline doctrine of the universality of sin safeguarded, is our next concern.

It may be something of a surprise to see St. Paul place such emphasis on original sin, which is after all something negative—something on which an apostle should apparently not want to dwell in his proclamation of the Good News. The herald of Jesus Christ should want to emphasize salvation—redemption, not sin. This is, of course, correct. Paul is not actually elaborating a dissertation on sin in his Letter to the Romans; he is insisting on our redemption from it. "The reason . . . why those who are in Christ Jesus are not condemned, is that the law of the spirit of life in Christ Jesus has set you free from the law of sin and death" (8:1).

So the positive side of these theologians' concern is the universal scope of Christ's redemptive act. As Paul says elsewhere, ". . . there is only one God, and there is only one mediator between God and mankind, himself a man, Christ

Jesus, who sacrificed himself as a ransom for them all"
(1 Tim 2:5). Salvation, the one thing that ultimately counts
in our human lives, is available nowhere other than in the
"name" (Person) of Jesus Christ. Of all the names in the
world given to persons, Peter insisted before the Sanhedrin,
"this is the only one by which we can be saved" (Acts 4:12).

Here we have the second obstacle, in the minds of the
doctrine's opponents, to its acceptance. And here we have
the second motive, in the minds even of many who accepted
it, for mitigating its obvious sense. Unless the Blessed
Virgin contracted original sin—or would have been infected
by it—or was supposed to contract it—or was supposed to
be included in Adam's headship so that she would have
contracted it—or has a "nature" that would have contracted it—then how could she be said to owe her salvation
to the "one mediator between God and humans"?

These are obviously valid, serious theological concerns:
the universality of original sin and the consequent universal
need for redemption from it through Jesus Christ alone, in
whose name alone we can be saved. Is it possible to safeguard the important doctrine in both these points and still
accept Pius IX's definition with an elegant, positive, absolute, and unmitigated literalness? We have already
hinted at the answer to this question. It is not only possible,
but necessary to do so. But it is also impossible to do so as
long as one maintains the Augustinian-Thomistic perspective on the divine creative plan. Bonnefoy has juxtaposed
sentences from the papal definition and an essay by a
twentieth-century Thomist in a striking illustration of the
conflict this perspective causes:

> Pius IX: "We define . . . that the most Blessed Virgin
> Mary . . . was preserved immaculate from all stain of
> original sin."

> Dominican Father Norbert del Prado: "The total
> preservation of the Blessed Virgin Mary from original
> sin seems to be contrary to Catholic Faith."[8]

Thus juxtaposed to the papal definition, del Prado's
contention appears shockingly heretical. But it must be
realized that the intention behind it is wholly praiseworthy
—that its author in no way intends to propound heresy,
and that he is struggling mightily to make sense of the
definition within a framework that does not allow him
to do so.

A reversal of the fundamental perspective accepted by
Thomas Aquinas is thus necessary for the literal acceptance
and full, proper understanding of the doctrine of Mary's
Immaculate Conception. This reversal is embodied in the
systematic synthesis we have used in earlier chapters of this
book. But it is one thing to see such a synthesis set forth
in wholly positive and speculative terms, and something
else again to assimilate it so that it pervades one's entire
theology and life. De Aldama, e.g., admits that one may
"defend the position that Mary was preserved from being
included in Adam." And there are some authors, he
continues,

> who try to suppress every obligation [to contract original
> sin] in Mary because they deny that she belonged to "the
> order of Adam" by reason of her predestination in
> Christ and with Christ prior to Adam. But it is not
> apparent in this viewpoint how one can retain a preserva-
> tive redemption from original sin,[9]

which de Aldama rightly sees as absolutely required by the
papal definition, according to which our Lady was "preserved immaculate from all stain of original sin . . . *in
virtue of the merits* of Jesus Christ."

According to the Scotistic framework of the Lord's absolute primacy in the creative plan, Mary was absolutely predestined to the hypostatic order in a "moment" of the creative decree *prior to* the establishment of the rest of the human race, and hence *prior to* its fall and consequent need for redemption. Now, there is nothing wrong with using the term "pre-redeem" to express what the Lord did for his mother, except that this term may appear to imply the need for rescue from some fate about to be actually incurred. On that account, it may be worth pointing out that Pius IX does not use the term at all, but rather the word "preserved." And in this word there is no implication at all that whatever fate Mary was "preserved from" is something that she "ought to," "should have," or "would have" incurred, any more than an infant "ought to have" tumbled out of his crib yet did not do so because there was a railing around it "preserving him from doing so." He need never have rolled anywhere near the edge of the crib.

Of course all analogies limp. In this case, the point of the analogy is that there need be no actual, positive tendency *toward* a danger for one to be "preserved from" that danger, and this is a valid observation. The *un*warranted comparison is that the railing does nothing positive for the infant, whereas Jesus does something, *every*thing, positive for Mary. It was out of love for him, in his humanity, that the Father created all things, including Mary, and that the Father bestowed every gift, including Mary's Immaculate Conception. Let us, at any rate, conclude that what the word "preserved" says is that Mary was "kept from" incurring original sin in the sense that it never had a chance to get near her. Instead of seeing the Lord's merits as warding off something that actually did tend to engulf her, let us see them as the positive source of her positive fullness of beauty and grace.

But as has been observed above, there is no way of making sense of this reversal of perspective as long as Mary is viewed as occupying a "moment" in the creative plan "after" Adam. Not only does Cardinal Suenens insist on viewing Mary in precisely this unfortunate way, asserting that "through sin, man spoilt [the] divine plan, but God . . . willed to transform his spoilt work into a new creation, of which Mary is the anticipation and the complete realization,"[10] but he introduces another interesting expedient in the form of a distinction between the natural and the supernatural orders. "What is involved here," he explains, "is an exception *in the order of grace.*" As far as the order of nature is concerned, "there is no question of Mary's being an exception . . . . She was conceived like every child of Adam, her divine Son only excepted, through the ordinary conjugal relation of her father and mother."[11]

We have already addressed the first of the author's points in explaining the Scotistic view of the divine plan. Adam did not, in that view, essentially "spoil" God's plan at all so as to cause, or even to occasion, the predestination of the Redeemer. Here we are concerned with his second point, according to which Mary is "conceived like every child of Adam" and is "no exception" to the general norm for mankind. This would be plausible if theology were an empirical science like biology. If it were only a question of examining the physical and biological facts of the case to attain a theological understanding of "the order of nature," we could easily conclude with Cardinal Suenens that the Blessed Virgin was, naturally speaking, merely a "child of Adam."

But theology is not biology, and its norms are not those of empirical generalization but rather revelation and careful logic. What belongs to the hypostatic order occurs in the divine plan "before," not after, the rest of creation.

The entire unfolding of history up to the visit paid by Gabriel to God's future Mother was absolutely and unconditionally intended to prepare for that visit. The election and predestination of the Blessed Virgin do not constitute an afterthought in the creative plan or make her an "exception" to anything that was originally planned.

The term "exception" is ill suited to the entire context, precisely because it presupposes the (by now almost universally discredited) Thomistic conception of the divine plan, according to which God was forced by sin to "modify" his original plan that made no provision for the Incarnation. In that view, everything connected with the Incarnation becomes an "exception" to or "revision" of what was originally supposed to be otherwise.

Equally unsuited to the context is another term used by Cardinal Suenens, when he says that "God has suspended by a miracle the hereditary contagion of original sin" in Mary's case.[12] A miracle is a sensibly perceptible exception to the ordinary course of nature, brought about by the direct intervention of divine power, and not one feature of this commonly accepted definition[13] applies to the Immaculate Conception. It is not a sensibly perceptible event; it is not an exception to the ordinary course of nature but is a primary feature of the creative plan establishing the course of nature; and it is not an "intervention" of God's power, but the realization of just what had been eternally and absolutely decreed to take place through that power.

It is not to be distastefully critical that we have spent so much time illustrating how pervasive and insidious the Thomistic preconception is, how it inevitably introduces contradictions, mistakes, and obfuscations into the best intended efforts to explain the Christian mysteries. Unfortunately, it is necessary to face these unpleasant facts if one is once for all going to give serious attention to the admittedly jarring and uncomfortable task of reversing completely the perspective that empirical observation and so-called "common sense" recommend to us.

If we can succeed in doing so; if the divine creative plan is understood as the consistent, single, comprehensive decree that must characterize the supremely intelligent Creator, one need no longer speak of "revisions," "exceptions," "obligations" to contract sin where none is contracted, or any other such ingenious but ultimately inviable devices. One is able to set forth in sheer simplicity and elegance a single, unified account of the predestination of the Blessed Virgin Mary from which there necessarily flows her Immaculate Conception precisely as that unique and blessed privilege was defined by Pope Pius IX.

As we have seen, the earliest Christians spoke spontaneously, if implicitly, of precisely that privilege. And they continued to do so throughout the ages, except in learned theological circles where Augustine's objections raised apparently insuperable difficulties. Not that Augustine's preoccupation with the universality of sin (against the Pelagians) and with the consequent universality of the need for redemption in Christ was unwarranted. On the contrary, his answer to the Pelagians was absolutely correct and exactly what was needed. But he did not, unfortunately, see that the Blessed Virgin Mary need never, should never, have been brought into the discussion. As a concluding summary of our discussion of the Immaculate Conception, let us make explicit the twofold justification of this assertion.

First, the universality of original sin. Augustine rightly insisted that every single human being under Adam's headship, without any exception, incurs the stain of original sin. Obscuring his consideration of this matter, however, was his overly physical interpretation of original sin itself, according to which it had to do with biological generation at least as much as moral inclusion under Adam's headship. But original sin is not a physical reality. Although it has certainly had its effects in the material order, it is in and of itself a moral reality which extends to Adam's progeny not on the basis of biological generation, but on the basis of humankind's corporate moral unity in Adam's headship. The Blessed Virgin Mary, however, predestined "before" Adam, is not, was not, and was not "supposed to have been" included in that moral unity. On the contrary, she belongs to the hypostatic order—the apex of the supernaturally permeated natural order which is the only one actually willed by God. From the viewpoint of the divine plan, as opposed to the empirical and historical viewpoint, Adam and all the rest of us are included under *her* and *her Son's* headship. The doctrine of the universality of original sin is therefore wholly irrelevant to a consideration of the essential reality of Mary's predestination,[14] and it holds no implications whatever for the doctrine of her Immaculate Conception.

Secondly, St. Augustine was also fully justified in his concern for the universality of redemption in Christ (we have seen the Pauline texts on which this concern is obviously based). But "redemption" strictly so called extends only as far as sin extends. Where there is no sin, there is no redemption in the strict sense. Preservation, we have pointed out, is not equivalent to redemption in this narrow sense which would imply the actual presence of, or "obligation to contract," sin. But the two do share something very important in common: both, like creation itself, are due to the Lord's meritorious causality. Thus the dogmatic definition of the Immaculate Conception states explicitly that Mary's "preservation" from sin—i.e., her fullness of grace and predestination to the hypostatic order where sin has no place—is due to "the merits of Jesus Christ." The essential meaning of the doctrine of universal redemption, which Augustine was quite properly concerned to defend, is that there is no life—we can add natural to Augustine's supernatural—no being whatever—for any creature apart from the incarnate Word's meritorious causality, in virtue of which the Creator has brought a universe into being and predestined it to attain its culmination in the Kingdom of the Lamb.

*NOTES*

# NOTES

## Chapter I

[1]See John E. Smith, *Experience and God* (New York: Oxford University Press, 1968), pp. 121-57, especially the concluding section on pp. 156-57.

[2]The reader interested in the history of this movement may wish to consult the anthology of essays by several of its prominent members, *The Revolution in Philosophy* (New York: St. Martin's Press, 1965).

[3]We shall return to this subject toward the end of our second chapter. The present reference is to Alfred North Whitehead, *Process and Reality* (New York: Harper & Row, 1929), p. 528.

[4]Without implying an unreserved or uncritical personal acceptance of Whitehead's entire doctrine of God by these authors and editors, we may refer the reader to the works in which they certainly propose the general adoption of Whiteheadian philosophy by Catholic theologians: Harry James Cargas and Bernard Lee, eds., *Religious Experience and Process Theology* (New York: Paulist Press, 1976); Bernard Lee, *The Becoming of the Church* (New York: Paulist Press, 1974); and Robert B. Mellert, *What Is Process Theology?* (New York: Paulist Press, 1975).

## Chapter II

[1]See Joseph M. Dalmau, S. J., "De Deo uno et trino," *Sacrae Theologiae Summa II* (Madrid: Biblioteca de Autores Cristianos, 1958), pp. 176-212, for a systematic treatment of predestination. Much of what follows here has been adapted from this treatise. The present reference is to p. 185.

²See the superb treatment of free choice and evil by Jacques Maritain in his book *Existence and the Existent*, trans. Lewis Galantiere and Gerald B. Phelan (Garden City, N.Y.: Doubleday-Image Books, 1956). pp. 94-99. On p. 98 Maritain says that the free creature "possesses the free initiative of an absence (or 'nothingness') of consideration, of a vacuum introduced into the warp and woof of being, of a *nihil . . . .*"

³For a straightforward discussion of Whitehead's concept of God, see Victor Lowe, *Understanding Whitehead* (Baltimore: Johns Hopkins Press, 1966), pp. 90-106. We say "straightforward," because Lowe does not attempt to take sides in the controversy over the proper understanding of God in Whitehead's system. On the contrary, clearly realizing that Whitehead himself "did not get all his insights adequately organized in his idea of God" and "wasn't primarily interested in God" (as Whitehead admitted to his student A. H. Johnson), Lowe wisely includes the topic of God under the general heading "philosophy of religion," in which Whitehead was in fact much more interested. Cf. A. H. Johnson, "Whitehead as Teacher and Philosopher," *Philosophy and Phenomenological Research* 29:3 (1969), 365.

The view that Whitehead's God is a single everlasting entity is held by Lewis S. Ford, in "The Non-Temporality of Whitehead's God," *International Philosophical Quarterly* 13 (1973), 347-76; and the opposite view, by John B. Cobb, Jr., in *A Christian Natural Theology* (Philadelphia: The Westminster Press, 1965), pp. 185-92.

⁴See Alfred North Whitehead, *Process and Reality*, p. 528.

⁵Lowe reports (op. cit., p. 106) that members of the audience at a lecture Whitehead gave on immortality left the hall where it was delivered asking one another, "Does he believe in immortality, or doesn't he?" In general, his followers are somewhat divided on the question. The utter disdain shown for the question by Donald W. Sherburne in "Responsibility, Punishment, and Whitehead's Theory of the Self," George L. Kline, ed., *Alfred North Whitehead: Essays on His Philosophy* (Englewood Cliffs, N.J.: Prentice Hall, 1963), pp. 179-88, seems most faithful to Whitehead's own attitude.

⁶For a concise explanation of Teilhard's use of the scientific evolutionary theory in his comprehensive outlook, see Joseph V. Kopp's booklet, *Teilhard de Chardin: A New Synthesis of Evolution* (New York: Paulist Press Deus Books, 1964).

⁷On Teilhard's metaphysics of creation, see Donald P. Gray, *The One and the Many: Teilhard de Chardin's Vision of Unity* (New York: Herder & Herder, 1969), especially pp. 15-33.

[8] On the world's consummation, see Teilhard de Chardin, *The Future of Man*, trans. Norman Denny (New York: Harper & Row Torchbooks, 1969), pp. 321-23. On the role of Jesus Christ in the evolutionary universe, see Teilhard's *Christianity and Evolution*, trans. René Hague (New York: Harcourt Brace Jovanovich, 1971).

[9] See, on Teilhard's devotion to our Lady, the chapter on "The Virgin Mary" in Henri de Lubac, *Teilhard de Chardin: The Man and His Meaning*, trans. René Hague (New York: New American Library Mentor-Omega Books, 1967), pp. 64-71.

[10] Such expressions pervade Teilhard's, *The Divine Milieu* (New York: Harper & Row, 1960) and *Hymn of the Universe* (New York: Harper & Row, 1965); but see his essay, "Pantheism and Christianity," in *Christianity and Evolution*, pp. 56-75.

[11] See Christopher F. Mooney, S. J., *Teilhard de Chardin and the Mystery of Christ* (New York: Harper & Row, 1964), especially the chapter on "The Redemption and the Mystery of Evil," pp. 104-45.

## Chapter III

[1] Cf. the discussion in the preceding chapter of Whiteheadian process Christology.

[2] See our review editorial, "Jesus and Process Philosophy," *The Cord* 24 (1974), 150-61; and David R. Griffin, "Faith, Reason, and Christology," ibid., 258-67. Readers who consult this discussion will find that we were unable to reach an understanding with Dr. Griffin; those who would like to evaluate his Christology for themselves should see especially pp. 167-92 of his book, *A Process Christology* (Philadelphia: Westminster Press, 1973).

[3] Dermot A. Lane, *The Reality of Jesus: An Essay in Christology* (New York: Paulist Press, 1977), pp. 109-29. See our review editorial of the book in *The Cord* 27 (1977), pp. 250; 278-80.

[4] Ibid., p. 113.

[5] Ibid., p. 112. What Father Lane has in mind is not the person as such, when he says it does not act, but the metaphysical abstraction, "subsistence," in virtue of which the person is autonomous, does not inhere in something else as, e.g., whiteness does in a white wall or humanity does in a human person.

[6]Rupert of Deutz, *De gloria et honore Filii Hominis*, Bk. 13, in Migne, *Patrologia Latina*, vol. 168, cols. 1624-29.

[7]Albert the Great, *In 3 Sent.*, d. 20, a. 4, in *Opera Omnia*, ed. Borgnet (Paris: Vivès, 1894), vol. 28, pp. 360-62.

[8]St. Thomas Aquinas, *Summa Theologica*, 3, 1, 3, in *Opera Omnia* (Rome: Vatican, 1903), vol. 11, pp. 13-14.

[9]Idem, *In I Tim.*, 1, lect. 4 (Parma: Fiaccadori, 1862), vol. 13, p. 590.

[10]Idem, *Summa*, 3, 1, 3, ad 4 (p. 14).

[11]John Duns Scotus, *Opus Oxoniense*, 3, d. 7, q. 3 (Paris: Vivès, 1894), vol. 14, pp. 348-60. A literal translation by Father Allan B. Wolter, O.F.M., has been published in *The Cord* 5 (1955), 369-72, and is preceded by a helpful if brief commentary.

[12]Scotus, like St. Thomas in his discussion of his fourth objection to the Lord's being predestined, used the Vulgate text. Instead of "predestined," the Jerusalem Bible has "proclaimed." Of course, if the Vulgate rendering is incorrect, the citation has no place at all in a consideration of this question.

[13]Bonnefoy wrote a good number of monographs on the Absolute Primacy of Jesus Christ and his Blessed Mother, culminating in his monumental work, *La primauté du Christ selon l'Ecriture et la tradition*, translated and edited by the present author as *Christ and the Cosmos* (Paterson, N.J.: St. Anthony Guild Press, 1965).

[14]St. Leo the Great, *Sermo I de Ascensione*, 2-4 (*PL* 54, 395-96), trans. in the new Office of Readings for Wednesday before the Ascension.

## Chapter IV

[1]Joseph A. de Aldama, S.J., "Mariologia," in *Sacrae Theologiae Summa* III (Madrid: Biblioteca de Autores Cristianos, 4th ed., 1961), pp. 325-481; L. J. Suenens, *Mary the Mother of God*, trans. by a Nun of Stanbrook Abbey; vol. 44 of the *Twentieth Century Encyclopedia of Catholicism* (New York: Hawthorn Books, 1959).

[2]De Aldama, p. 334.

[3]Suenens, p. 20.

[4]Ibid., p. 21.

[5]Duns Scotus, loc. cit., trans. Wolter, p. 371.

⁶To avoid the impression of a contradiction between this statement
and Duns Scotus's assertion that Jesus [and Mary] are first predestined
to "glory" by the Agent who works in an orderly fashion, let us note
that two rather different perspectives are involved. Scotus's point
remains correct. Within Mary's overall destiny, glory is the end to be
attained, and therefore the "first" moment of her predestination. But
here we are concerned, not with the moments of the decree predestining
Mary in its complete structure, but more specifically with the predefined
actions included in that decree as related to other creatures. Which of
her actions, we are asking, is fundamental to the concrete working out
of her predestination to glory? And the answer is, her role as Mother of
the Incarnate Word.

⁷There were several junctures in the course of this book where we
could have raised the question of the reason for God's permitting sin
at all, and its implications for the Incarnation. Feeling that an adequate
discussion of this issue would upset the balance of our presentation and
be out of place in so brief an essay, we have up to now avoided it. It does
seem necessary here, however, at least to mention that explanations
have in fact been given which do not compromise the assertion being
made here to the effect that sin does not condition the Incarnation. Two
of them, in fact, go so far as to insist that not only the Incarnation itself,
but even its redemptive mode—i.e., the actual coming of Christ precisely
as Suffering Servant, as Redeemer—is unconditioned by sin. Just the
opposite: in decreeing the Incarnation as his first and greatest work,
God took into account the various ways in which it might be accom-
plished and, without in any way approving of sin, actually provided for
the redemptive Incarnation as the path Jesus was to follow to glory.
M. J. Scheeben suggests that this redemptive modality enables Jesus
to exercise more fully his mediative power than would the mere dis-
tribution of God's gifts in a sinless universe (*The Mysteries of Christianity*, trans. Cyril Vollert [St. Louis: B. Herder, 1946], pp. 399-400).
Bonnefoy's explanation emphasizes the Lord's love, rather than his
power. Playing on the term "pardon," he suggests that the prefix *par*
implies, in virtue of its root Latin meaning, "fullness" or "perfection."
The stem *don*, meaning gift, is thus intensified by the prefix: "pardon"
is the perfect or supreme gift, and the Lord is enabled to bestow it through
his redemptive suffering (Bonnefoy, *The Immaculate Conception in
the Divine Plan*, trans. M. D. Meilach, O.F.M. [Paterson, N.J.: St.
Anthony Guild Press, 1967], pp. 28-31. This explanation is lavishly
embellished in Bonnefoy's larger work, *Christ and the Cosmos*, through
the skillful use of such insights as the Lord's own insistence that only by
dying can the seed bring forth new life (Jn 12:24-25).

Aware that Bonnefoy's position is startling to readers who come upon it for the first time, Father Juniper B. Carol, O.F.M., seeks to reassure them: "We need not be shocked at the above explanation of the permission of sin. St. Paul himself endorses it when he writes: 'For God shut up all in unbelief, so that he may have mercy on all'" ("Reflections on the Problem of Mary's Preservative Redemption," *Marian Studies* 30 [1979], 19-88; p. 75).

[8]For a systematic discussion of the Coredemption within the framework of our Lady's absolute predestination, see the author's article, "Standing by the Cross of Jesus," *Interest* (Washington, D.C.: Holy Name College) 1:6 (Summer, 1962), 5-17. Pp. 15-17 of the article contain an extensive bibliography on the subject. Discussing the difficulties caused for Protestant thinkers by the title Coredemptrix, Father Eamon R. Carroll, O. Carm., makes two main points. First, he sets forth the term's meaning as we have done here, showing its orthodox character. Then, in the second place, he calls attention to the ecumenical concerns of the Second Vatican Council, which led the conciliar Fathers to "eliminate some of the ecumenical offense it saw" in the terminology exemplified by the title Coredemptrix (*Understanding the Mother of Jesus* [Wilmington, DE: Michael Glazier, Inc., 1979], pp. 95-96). We do not fully sympathize with this position for reasons akin to those furnished in our earlier discussion of the person-nature terminology used to express the doctrine of the Incarnation. This title says something very precise. One may consider it excessive to call *every* Christian a "coredeemer," which is exactly what St. Paul envisages in Col 1:24, without using the term. But the unique sublimity of our Lady's role, we feel, warrants the explicit use of the term Coredemptrix. The Incarnation, we explained, is so different from any other reality that whatever terms we chose to substitute for "person" and "nature" would need as much explanation as they do before their meaning as applied to the Incarnation could be clear. Similarly here, no one else is the "beloved Associate of Christ," or the sinless Mother who bore him. No one else contributed to the universal objective redemption to the degree that she did; and we feel that the term Coredemptrix is admirably suited to stress the unique role she played and continues to play in humankind's salvation.

[9]St. Albert the Great, *In 1 Sent.*, d. 44, a. 5, ad 3, cited by de Aldama, p. 327. (Receptive to God: Latin, *capax Dei*.)

[10]The principle is cited here as furnished by de Aldama, ibid.

[11]René Laurentin, "Mary and the Feminist Movement," part 2, *The Queen* 29:5 (Jan.-Feb., 1979), 7-17.

[12]John de Satge, *Down to Earth: The New Protestant Vision of the Virgin Mary* (Wilmington, NC: McGrath Publishing Company Consortium Books, 1976), p. 68. The author, clearly uneasy with the traditional Roman Catholic conceptual framework, still elaborates a remarkable "theological life of Mary" (pp. 74-79) as prototype of the Church and of humankind.

## Chapter V

[1]Pius IX, *Ineffabilis Deus*, English translation by Dominic J. Unger, O.F.M. Cap., *Mary Immaculate* (Paterson, NJ: St. Anthony Guild Press, 1946), p. 21.

[2]Pius IX, ibid.; Pius XII, *Munificentissimus Deus, Acta Apostolicae Sedis* 32 (1950), 768, cited by de Aldama, p. 342. We stress these two popes because of the renown of the two Marian documents in which they provide this interpretation of the biblical texts cited here. To them we can add, with de Aldama, Leo XIII, St. Pius X, and Pius XI (ibid).

[3]De Aldama, p. 344; further references omitted in the following historical sketch can be found here and on succeeding pages in de Aldama's tract.

[4]In an evolutionary interpretation of creation, there may or may not be a single human couple at the time of humankind's emergence. Many scientists consider the possibility of the whole race's descent from such a single couple extremely remote. Whatever is to be said of this question, however, we have no choice theologically but to admit universal contamination of the first generation of human beings by original sin, which was then transmitted to all their descendants. See the somewhat ambivalent discussion of this matter by Piet Schoonenberg, *God's World in the Making* (Pittsburgh: Duquesne University Press, 1964), pp. 83-85; the same author's much more extensive treatment, *Man and Sin: A Theological View*, trans. J. Donceel, S.J. (Notre Dame: Notre Dame University Press, 1965); and Robert T. Francoeur, *Perspectives in Evolution* (Baltimore: Helicon Press, 1965). pp. 185-229.

[5]See Bonnefoy, *The Immaculate Conception . . .*, p. 40.

[6]Ibid., p. 41.

[7]See ibid., p. 55.

[8]Ibid., p. 48.

[9]De Aldama, p. 352.

[10]Suenens, p. 30.

[11]Ibid., p. 27.

[12]Ibid., p. 31.

[13]Cf. Michael Nicolau, S.J., "De Revelatione Christiana sive de vera religione," *Sacrae Theologiae Summa* I (Madrid: Biblioteca de Autores Cristianos, 1965), p. 161.

[14]We say, a consideration of "the essential reality" because the Incarnation is evidently redemptive in its *modality*. Cf. above, Chapter IV, note 7, where a brief explanation is given of two ways to contend that the divine provision for sin and redemption within the creative plan is itself ordained to the Lord's greater glory and that of his Blessed Mother.